Sharpen Your Sword

A Seven-Week Devotional Study to Walk Confidently in Your Identity in Christ

JOANNE DELANOY

WESTBOW PRESS®
A DIVISION OF THOMAS NELSON
& ZONDERVAN

Cover Design: Robynn Lang, Donazon Van Raamsdonk, Joanne Delanoy
Graphics (cover and interior): Robynn Lang
Cover photos: Donazon Van Raamsdonk, Joanne Delanoy
Author photo: Donazon Van Raamsdonk

WestBow Press books may be ordered through booksellers or by contacting:

WestBow Press
A Division of Thomas Nelson & Zondervan
1663 Liberty Drive
Bloomington, IN 47403
www.westbowpress.com
1 (866) 928-1240

ISBN: 978-1-5127-7761-1 (sc)
ISBN: 978-1-5127-7762-8 (hc)
ISBN: 978-1-5127-7760-4 (e)

Library of Congress Control Number: 2017902979

Print information available on the last page.

WestBow Press rev. date: 5/23/2017

Dedication

To my Lord and Savior, Jesus Christ—this has been your project right from the beginning. It has been a huge honor to partner with you in this venture. In our short time together there have already been so many adventures and I look forward to many more to come! I came across this poem that I wrote to you at the beginning of 2013 while we were on one of our early adventures together—my first time leading a Bible study. It is just as relevant, if not more so, today as it was then.

> I love you God, with all my heart,
>   And you loved me from the very start.
> You patiently loved me all these years,
>   Even while I gave in to my worldly fears.
> You have given me infinite mercy and grace,
>   I can't wait to meet you face to face.
> Until that time, I will spend my life
>   Honoring your ultimate sacrifice!

To my precious daughter, Danielle—you have changed my life in countless ways. I am so blessed, honored, and grateful that God chose me to be your mom. I love you deeply and I am so proud of who you are.

To my mom and dad, Blanche and Larry, thank you for your love and support. It means the world to me, as do both of you. I love you!

Contents

Acknowledgements

There are so many people who have taught, coached, mentored, supported, and encouraged me in my journey of faith. I can't possibly list all of them so I would like to start by thanking everybody who has walked with me in some capacity on this journey. Every divine connection has been significant!

To Mike and Monica Prescott, thank you for your obedience and perseverance in starting City Life Church almost twenty-five years ago. My life and Danielle's life are two of the countless lives that have been transformed as a result of your dedication, faith, courage, and leadership. I am forever thankful!

I would also like to thank my entire City Life Church family—life with all of you is such a blessing!

To my beautiful daughter, Danielle Choquette, thank you for being you. Your courage and boldness are admirable, and it is these qualities that ultimately led me to City Life and to Jesus. I was once asked to write my testimony in six words, these are the words I chose: Daughter led me, Jesus consumed me. For this I am eternally grateful. I love you with all my heart!

Monica, I would like to also thank you for inviting me to be part of your discipleship group in 2012—it changed the trajectory of my life. And a special thank you to all the women who were in that group—Kristine, Dawn, Robynn, Larissa, Amanda, Amy, Erin, Leanna, Jana, and Sarah. That was a time of huge growth and the relationships that were formed have been a significant part of my journey. Although some of the learning was tough, I will always remember that time fondly.

Janet Little, thank you for your friendship and mentorship these past few years. You model what it means to walk with Jesus. Thank you for loving me enough to gently, and not so gently when required, guide me as I learned to recognize and follow God's voice, and for coaching me and encouraging me to make this project a priority.

Karen Wall and Colleen Hancar, thank you for your friendship, support, kind words of encouragement, and prayers.

To the She Speaks United group—Taylor, Danielle, Kristine, Jen, Jessica, Lindsay, Carrie-Sam, Amber, and Kathy Jo—thank you for helping me to find my voice. I am forever grateful for your love, encouragement, and wisdom.

Jen Blackwood, thank you for cheering me on! You continually boost me and energize me with your uplifting and motivating words and your belief in me. You are a precious gem and I am so thankful for you!

Irene Reid, thank you for being such an inspiration! You are an example of God's promise in Psalm 103:5—you have shown that following Jesus renews our youth like the eagle's. I pray that *Sharpen Your Sword* will help people of all ages rise up to be a mighty warrior of God, like you are.

I would also like to give a shout out to Tanya Anderson for assisting me with the title of the book. Thank you for your honesty and insight!

Of course, I could not do a project like this on my own. Thank you to Robynn Lang for her valuable insight and feedback on the content and format of the book, and for her amazing cover design and graphics. Donazon Van Raamsdonk, thank you for your creativity and input into the cover design as well as your stellar photography skills. And thank you to Liz Zook for the tedious task of editing my manuscript. I greatly appreciate your patience and your expertise to improve the final product and make it the best it could be!

Foreword

I remember very clearly the first Sunday Joanne came to City Life Church. As a pastor, you tend to meet a wide variety of people on Sundays, everyone at different stages in their journey. But it's the ones who found the courage to walk through the doors of church for the first time that tend to stand out: they tend to come away with what we affectionately refer to as the "deer in headlights" look because our gatherings tend to be very different than what people typically expect of church.

Except for Joanne.

She had a bit of the deer in headlights look but there was something else very evident: the deep look of someone pondering, someone taking it all in; someone with a mix of "not quite sure" but also hunger. A hunger that I have watched over the years grow from being a hunger and thirst for knowledge to become a ravenous craving to know the Giver of Truth, the One Who reveals to us who we truly are. And I know this is Joanne's heart for you as you take your own journey through *Sharpen Your Sword*.

I'm a firm believer that there is so much of life that is caught more than it is taught. As you read through *Sharpen Your Sword* I hope you will catch the same passionate hunger and surrender that has fuelled Joanne's own journey in getting to know her Savior and that like her, you'll discover and embrace the real you He knows and longs for you to know too.

Monica Prescott
Lead Pastor
City Life Church – Leduc, Alberta, Canada

Introduction

I have the best conversations with God when I am walking outside in His creation, with the sun on my face, the fresh air in my lungs, and His beauty displayed all around me! This is often when I hear from Him the most clearly. This book is a result of one of those walks. The Holy Spirit downloaded to me what He wanted me to do with some of the many things that He has been teaching me on my journey of faith. I started writing as soon as I got home!

There are so many elements to our faith journey; so many areas of growth and learning. Second Corinthians 5:17 tells us that in Christ we are a new creation, that the old is gone and the new is here. For some people, this new creation is evident immediately. For others, the outward transformation is a slower process.

We are three-part beings: we have a spirit, soul, and body. When we accept Jesus Christ as our Lord and Savior, our spirit comes to life, it is born (hence the term "born again"). However, our soul—which is our mind, will and emotions—and our body are still the same. Depending on how long we have lived prior to accepting Christ and depending on our life experiences, our body and soul could have a lot of baggage that needs to be cleaned out. To be led by the Holy Spirit in our daily living, we need to feed our spirit so that it becomes bigger than both our body (physical cravings) and our soul (mind, will and emotions). Prior to our spirit being born, it is our body and soul that lead us in our decisions, thoughts, behaviors and actions. Growing our spirit to be the largest of our three-part being, will allow the Holy Spirit to lead us in our decisions, thoughts, behaviors, and actions. This growth process is called sanctification.

My heart for this book is for it to be a tool that assists you in your sanctification process; that helps grow your spirit and deepen your relationship with Jesus Christ. I pray that it will help you develop a hunger and thirst for God's Word that is insatiable! I believe that it is only through developing a relationship with Jesus Christ that we will truly get a heart transformation rather than just a behavior modification. It is transformation that allows us to live in the fruit of the Spirit: "love, joy, peace, patience, kindness, goodness, faithfulness, gentleness and self-control" (Galatians 5:22–23). And it is through this transformation that others will be drawn to know our Lord and Savior, Jesus Christ.

From a practical sense, I hope that this book will help you to develop a devotional discipline that grows your love and knowledge of the Bible and enhances your prayer life. In addition, it can be a tool that helps you discover a journaling style that suits you; one that you can incorporate into your regular time with God. Journaling is not only helpful in capturing and reflecting on what you are learning (additional insight is often revealed to me as I am journaling), but it also keeps a record for reference. This will be useful when you need a reminder of what you have learned. It can also be useful as a reference to help others in their journey. When God reveals something to us, it is not just meant for us, it is always meant to help others as well. The exact details of your circumstance will not always be meant for sharing, but the lessons learned will always be helpful to those that are in situations that require the same lessons. God will use what you learned to help them apply it to their circumstance. We can only do this if we remember those lessons!

I pray that this book will deepen your relationship with Jesus Christ; that you will come to know Him more intimately. It is only through knowing Him that true transformation will occur and bring peace that surpasses all understanding. And with this transformed heart, you will be able to walk boldly and confidently in your identity in Christ—spreading the aroma of Him wherever you go!

How to Use This Devotional Study

This devotional study has been separated into specific topic areas. The first time through I recommend starting at the beginning and working your way through each topic. After that, each topic can be used separately as desired.

Within every topic, there will be several days of devotions that will build upon each other. Interspersed among the devotions will be *Transformational Tips* to provide practical tools you can apply to your life to grow in that area of your faith journey.

Each day there will be a couple of questions to help provide deeper introspection. In addition, there will be space available for you to journal any revelations, thoughts, or ideas that God has provided during your devotional time. This space was intentionally left without lines to allow freedom in your journaling style. Some prefer to journal in sentence format, while others may prefer to draw pictures, use bullet points, or mind mapping techniques. If you don't know what your style is, I encourage you to experiment with a variety of journaling styles. You can even create your own style! It doesn't matter how you do it, just start capturing your thoughts in whatever way comes to you.

Once you have had time to reflect and capture your revelations, then you can identify any specific areas that you would like to circle in prayer. Simply write the topic of prayer within the circle, and—if required—provide a detailed description (you should have enough information to remind you of the specifics to pray for). Mark Batterson explains the legend of Honi the circle maker in his book titled *The Circle Maker*. During a great drought in 100 BC, Honi drew a circle on the ground and swore to God that he would not leave that circle until He had shown them mercy with rain—and God responded. The book goes on to tell us: "The circle he drew in the sand became a sacred symbol. And the legend of Honi the circle maker stands forever as a testament to the power of a single prayer to change the course of history."[1] The circles in which you will write your prayers are symbols to remind you of the power of prayer and to keep praying until God answers.

If you would like to go a little deeper, you can find a Bible verse to go with each prayer—this verse can be used as part of your prayer. There are many tools that can be used to find Bible verses to support your prayer. Depending on your Bible, there may be a concordance at the back of the Bible to look up various topics. In addition, biblegateway.com or blueletterbible.org are good websites that can be used to search for Bible verses. I also find google.com to be a very useful tool when searching for various types of verses; the search doesn't have to be as specific as it does when using the aforementioned sites. I also highly recommend the books: *The Secret Power of Speaking God's Word* by Joyce Meyer, and *Praying God's Word: Breaking Free from Spiritual Strongholds* by Beth Moore. These are great books to help you pray Scripture regarding specific topics.

LOVE

God's Love for You

In the spring of 2014, I felt God calling me to end my profession of twenty-eight years and go to Bible college. I was confident that this was what He wanted me to do. So I applied immediately and even ended up handing in my resignation at my place of employment before I was officially accepted. Although this is not necessarily the approach I would recommend to everyone, I have a habit of overanalyzing things and I didn't want to allow time for doubt to settle in and convince myself that I hadn't heard God correctly or that it wasn't God I had heard at all. At that time, I knew with every fiber of my being that this was what God wanted me to do. I was covered in a blanket of peace—the peace that surpasses understanding. So, at the age of forty-seven, I was off to Bible college!

What I learned and experienced during that year of Bible college could be a whole book in itself, but today I will share with you the most significant revelation I had about myself. I find that God often teaches me the most through things that I don't think apply to me. This was no exception. During our women's small group, one of the ladies in the group started discussing a book that was written by one of our teachers who was also a pastor at the church where I was attending college. The book is titled *I Don't Think So* by Melanie Mitchell. When I saw that the book was about overcoming a victim mentality, I thought it didn't apply to me because I didn't have a victim mentality. In fact, victim mentalities are one of my pet peeves—so surely this book would not be relevant to me. But I did want to read the book since my teacher had written it. I thought maybe I could learn something that I could pass along to someone else. Before I even got a chance to buy the book, a beautiful young lady in my class purchased it for me! So I had no excuse—I needed to read the book.

As I was reading the chapter titled *Uncovering the Lies*, I read a question that knocked the wind out of me and left me reeling. I became a sobbing, weeping, puddle on the floor as I realized the fundamental root cause of my beliefs, thoughts, actions, and relationships. The question was only seven words: "Who told you that you were unlovable?"[2]

When I read that question, I realized I believed I was unlovable.

The book went on to say in another chapter, "People who believe they are rejected are unable to receive love, even though that is what they desperately want. They are convinced they are unlovable, so when someone demonstrates love toward them, it is almost impossible for them to receive it...Or they believe it is just a matter of time until the other person realizes they are unworthy of love or affection. As a result, they respond to love, affection, and generosity by trying to repay it."[3]

I unknowingly took this belief into my relationship with Jesus: focusing on my love for Him rather than His love for me. I believed in His love for others, but I hadn't realized that I didn't believe in His love for *me*.

I unintentionally continued in the life-long pattern of working hard and trying to be perfect because I thought that love and acceptance were based on what I did.

This revelation occurred in November of 2014. The focus word that I chose for 2015 was "love" (if you aren't familiar with the concept of a focus word, I will touch more on it later). I decided I would seek and study about God's love for me. My memory verses, my Bible study, and the books I read revolved around that theme. Much of the material used within this section comes from what I learned or relearned in a new way through that year of focus.

My theme verse for the year (and for this section of the devotional study) was Ephesians 3:17–19:

> And I pray that you, being rooted and established in love, may have power, together with all the Lord's holy people, to grasp how wide and long and high and deep is the love of Christ, and to know this love that surpasses knowledge—that you may be filled to the measure of all the fullness of God.

Maybe you are like I was and have trouble believing in His love for you. You feel you need to earn God's love, or you may not even realize that you have this inaccurate belief. But even if you do believe in God's love for you, don't skip this section; God will still speak to you to strengthen your bond with Him.

It was only when I realized God's love for me specifically that I could open up my heart and let Him in. Before, I was keeping Him at a distance as someone whom I loved and admired from afar, but whom I wouldn't let get too close for fear that I would get rejected. When the walls around my heart started to come down, His love flooded in! That is when true healing could begin. It is believing in His love for me that allows me to trust Him completely and know Him more intimately—deepening our relationship.

Accepting God's love for you is *fundamental* in your faith journey. I pray as you read and meditate on this section, your realization and acceptance of God's love for you will deepen and you will be filled to the measure of all the fullness of God.

Love—Day 1

We live in a society that uses the word "love" flippantly. We *love* food, athletes, celebrities, sports, art, TV shows, movies, and the list goes on. We use the word so often it has lost its significance. We use the same word to describe our feelings for soft toilet paper as we do our feelings for God Almighty, the Creator of heaven and earth!

Not only that, but as soon as a new and improved version of the toilet paper comes out, our *love* shifts from the old to the new. Or, when a celebrity we *love* does something that makes loving him or her look bad, we abandon that *love* and move on to the next up-and-coming reality star. This leaves us with a warped idea of love—we consciously or subconsciously (I think most often the latter) think that love is erratic, unreliable, inconsistent, and temporary.

In addition to promoting a watered-down, disillusioned, weakened meaning of love, society has defined value based on popularity, achievements, wealth, and status.

This combination has us striving to gain our value through performance, position, and material possessions so that we will be acceptable enough to be loved. It is no wonder we have trouble comprehending God's never-ending, never-changing, never-failing love for us!

As we embark on our journey to discover or deepen our understanding of God's love for us, it is important to have an accurate definition of love. The best place to find that definition is in God's Word. First Corinthians 13:4–8 gives a great foundational definition of love on which we can start our journey:

> Love is patient, love is kind. It does not envy, it does not boast, it is not proud. It does not dishonor others, it is not self-seeking, it is not easily angered, it keeps no record of wrongs. Love does not delight in evil but rejoices with the truth. It always protects, always trusts, always hopes, always perseveres. Love never fails.

Describe one experience that you've had that may have skewed your perception of love.

How do you feel about God's love for you? Do you believe it? Do you have any problems accepting it?

How do your feelings about His love for you align with the definition from 1 Corinthians?

Journal any additional messages, thoughts, or ideas that God has placed on your heart:

Prayer Circles

Based on your revelations, reflections, thoughts, and ideas, what or whom can you circle in prayer?

Details: Details:

Bible Verse: Bible Verse:

Love—Day 2

Society has fed us a lie that we gain our value through performance, position, and material possessions. The truth is:

You are *not* what you do.

You are *not* what you have done in the past or what somebody else has done to you.

You are *not* where you live or how much money you make.

You are *not* what others say or think about you.

You are *not* even what you think about yourself.

Your value is not based on any of these things. If you want to know who you are, then you need to ask the *One* who created you! Your value is based on who you are in Christ; you are who God says you are. In order to know who He says you are, you need to look to His Word.

This is what He says:

But you are a chosen people, a royal priesthood, a holy nation, God's special possession, that you may declare the praises of him who called you out of darkness into his wonderful light. (1 Peter 2:9)

You are *chosen*, He picked you specifically, you are not an accident; He has a specific plan and purpose for you (Jeremiah 29:11).

You are *royalty*, a child of the King of kings; you are a prince or princess anointed to perform sacred duties (Isaiah 61:1).

You are *holy*; through Jesus Christ, you are the righteousness of God (2 Corinthians 5:21).

You are *God's special possession*. The Greek word for *possession* means "to preserve for one's self."[4] You are precious to Him, and He chose you to be His very own; He wants to protect you, and He holds you in the palm of His hand (Isaiah 41:10).

Read the scriptures that are listed. Which one is speaking to you the most and why?

What is the lie that you need to replace with truth?

Journal any additional messages, thoughts, or ideas that God has placed on your heart:

Prayer Circles

Based on your revelations, reflections, thoughts, and ideas, what or whom can you circle in prayer?

Details: Details:

Bible Verse: Bible Verse:

Transformational Tip #1: Know God's Word

To really know this love, you need to know Jesus, and to know Jesus—you need to know the Word. Jesus is the Word made flesh (John 1:14). You need to memorize, meditate, and study the Word of God so you have it hidden in your heart (Psalm 119:11). The word "study" does not have to be intimidating: It does not mean that you have to become a theologian or a Hebrew and Greek linguist. *Study* simply means "to read carefully or intently, to think deeply, reflect or consider."[5] Basically, it is to think about what you are reading and to give it careful consideration instead of quickly reading through it. Having other people tell you what the Bible says through messages at church, or at conferences, or on podcasts is good—but it is not the same as reading it yourself. You will not get nearly the same impact that you will get from reading and deliberating on it alone with just you and the Holy Spirit, who is our greatest Teacher. Hearing the Word from others will give you the intellectual knowledge to know what it says, but you won't get the same experiential/relational knowledge of who Jesus is.

> But the Advocate, the Holy Spirit, whom the Father will send in my name, will teach you all things and will remind you of everything I have said to you. (John 14:26)

When I had to take a Bible Memory class in Bible college, I was scared. I didn't think I could do it. My memory was not the same as it used to be and I feared failure. What I learned through that class is that God will give you the grace you need to accomplish His plans. The more you read the Bible, the easier it becomes to remember. I don't always remember the verses word for word, but I remember the key points. Do not believe the lie that you cannot memorize Scripture. That is exactly what Satan wants you to believe.

When you have God's Word in your memory bank, it becomes a powerful weapon when you need to withdraw it to fight against the lies of the enemy, your own thoughts, or the inaccurate ideals and beliefs perpetrated by society.

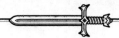

For the next week, focus on the verse above, John 14:26, and commit it to memory. Read it over and over. Record it on the voice recorder on your phone (or another device) and listen to it repeatedly. There are even memorization apps you can download that will play the recording over and over until you stop it. Memorize it to a melody or use actions. Anything that works for you. You can do it!

Find a Bible reading plan that works for you. Don't worry about getting through the entire Bible in a certain period of time. Instead, focus on consistently reading at least a small portion (even one verse) every day.

Love—Day 3

As God's cherished possession, He wants to protect you.

In John 17:11, Jesus prays to His Father to protect you by the power of His name:

> I will remain in the world no longer, but they are still in the world, and I am coming to you. Holy Father, *protect* them by the power of your name, the name you gave me, so that they may be one as we are one.

First John 5:18 states: "The One who was born of God *keeps* them safe, and the evil one cannot harm them." (Emphasis mine in both verses.)

The Greek word that is used for both *protect* and *keeps* in the above verses is *tereo* (tā-re'-ō), which means: "to attend to carefully, to guard, to take care of."[6] And the root words of *tereo* mean: "to enjoy the presence of one, to behold, look upon, view attentively, of important persons that are looked on with admiration."[7]

Jesus takes care of you! He enjoys your presence! He carefully attends to you. He looks upon you attentively with admiration as an important person.

The Lord knit you together in your mother's womb so He can delight in you. You are His precious child, greatly loved and dear to His heart.

Which definition of *tereo* resonates in your heart? Is there one that speaks the most to you? If so, why does it stand out to you?

How does it make you feel that God admires *you* as an important person; that He enjoys you and delights in you? Do you believe it? Can you accept His admiration?

Journal any additional messages, thoughts, or ideas that God has placed on your heart:

Prayer Circles

Based on your revelations, reflections, thoughts, and ideas, what or whom can you circle in prayer?

Details: Details:

Bible Verse: Bible Verse:

Love—Day 4

You are God's creation! His masterpiece! In Psalm 139, David was praising God for the way He created him. David was acknowledging that he was fearfully and wonderfully made because of Who made him. God doesn't make mistakes! You are not a mistake! You are the handiwork of our Almighty Creator! The same God that created heaven and earth, created you. He knows every hair on your head (Matthew 10:30) and He has engraved you on the palms of His hands (Isaiah 49:16). Let your doubts and fears drift away as you meditate on the scripture below. Let it sink in and penetrate your heart.

> For you created my inmost being; you knit me together in my mother's womb. I praise you because I am fearfully and wonderfully made; your works are wonderful, I know that full well. My frame was not hidden from you when I was made in the secret place. When I was woven together in the depths of the earth, your eyes saw my unformed body. All the days ordained for me were written in your book before one of them came to be. (Psalm 139:13–16)

While in Bible college, I was learning to study the Bible by doing more in-depth study of the words, including the Hebrew and Greek meanings. During that time, as part of my own practice, I studied all the key words in the above verses and wrote my own translation based on the definitions found in that word study. I used this exercise to help me meditate on the meaning of this scripture; to let a deeper meaning fill my heart. I have shared it with you in the hopes that it will do the same for you.

Psalm 139:13–16 (Joanne's translation):

Lord, Your creations, accomplishments and achievements surpass my understanding. Your works are marvelous, extraordinary, miraculous; and I am no exception. You have made me worthy of honor and respect, to be revered. You set me apart to be distinguished and distinct. You formed me and protected me to be a vessel that is complete and made perfect in Jesus Christ. My soul is a fire that is stirred up and comes ablaze in awe of all your wonderful works. You were fully aware of the power and might that You were creating in the shelter of my mother's womb. You gave special attention to my creation to make me unique, to vary my appearance and to skillfully mold me as a diverse and humble asset for the sake of the whole earth. You eagerly anticipated the enjoyment of our relationship. The vast, spacious life You offer me was engraved in Your book before I ever came to be.

What would your translation be? Write your own prayer to God based on what Psalm 139:13–16 means to you. You may want to use this prayer as one of your prayer circles today.

Journal any additional messages, thoughts, or ideas that God has placed on your heart:

Prayer Circles

Based on your revelations, reflections, thoughts, and ideas, what or whom can you circle in prayer?

Details: Details:

Bible Verse: Bible Verse:

Transformational Tip #2: Pray Scripture (Out Loud)

Prayer is powerful. Praying using Scripture will add another level of depth to your prayers. And to go to yet another level, pray it out loud. This adds authority and will ignite your faith! God's Word does not come back empty; it will achieve the purpose for which He sent it (Isaiah 55:11). God gave us His Word to show us who He is. Praying His words and His promises will reveal His character more and more, growing an intimate knowledge and a personal relationship.

Prayer is an essential communication tool to get to know God. Often we use prayer as one-way communication, asking God for help or thanking Him and praising Him. All of those are good things and very necessary in your prayer life, but prayer is also a way for God to speak to you. Allow times of silence during your personal prayer time for God to respond. Be ready to listen. It is a two-way conversation. We can't get to know somebody better if we are always the one doing the talking.

I think the best place to start praying Scripture is in the Book of Psalms, which is a book of prayers that were put to music and sung as hymns. King David wrote a large portion of the Book of Psalms and he poured out his heart to God in all situations, good or bad (you can find David's story in 1 and 2 Samuel and the beginning of 1 Kings). No matter what your circumstance, I am certain there is a Psalm that will speak to you and what you are currently experiencing.

There are also a couple of books that I have found very powerful and helpful when it comes to praying Scripture and I highly recommend having them available in your arsenal of resources: Beth Moore's book, *Praying God's Word: Breaking Free from Spiritual Strongholds*, uses Scripture as personalized prayers for specific strongholds such as rejection, addiction, insecurity, pride, unbelief, and many more; Joyce Meyer's book, *The Power of Speaking God's Word*, is a pocket-size book that can easily be carried with you. It is categorized into topics such as anger, jealousy, fear, pride, loneliness, etc., so that you can easily find scriptures for whatever you need in the moment.

Find a Psalm that speaks to the current season that you are in and pray it out loud. It may feel uncomfortable at first but be persistent. Pray it again. Then listen for God's response.

The response may be a specific thought, or idea or it could be a feeling of peace, or renewed strength. Often we receive responses a little at a time. Additional responses are revealed in a variety of ways as we are ready for them. Keep your eyes, ears, and heart open to receive in the days, weeks, and months ahead.

Love—Day 5

As part of our human nature, it is difficult for us to accept that God loves us so deeply. Because the love of human beings is limited, our minds and our hearts struggle to grasp the limitless love of our Creator. We expect conditions. We base our worthiness of love on what we have done or not done. We feel we need to earn it; that we don't deserve it otherwise. I am so thankful that God's ways are not our ways and His thoughts are not our thoughts—that they are so much higher (Isaiah 55:8–9)!

The Bible tells us we are more than conquerors and that nothing in all creation will be able to separate us from the love of God that is in Christ Jesus our Lord.

I like the way *The Message* paraphrases it:

> None of this fazes us because Jesus loves us. I'm absolutely convinced that nothing—nothing living or dead, angelic or demonic, today or tomorrow, high or low, thinkable or unthinkable—absolutely *nothing* can get between us and God's love because of the way that Jesus our Master has embraced us. (Romans 8:37–39 MSG)

Often, "religious" thinking can cause us to believe that we cannot talk to God until we somehow make ourselves worthy. It is so important to realize that there is nothing *you* can do to make yourself worthy. You are worthy because God loves you! In fact, He loves you so much that He sent His Son to die on the cross for your sins (1 John 4:10). Jesus came to restore your relationship with God because there is nothing that you can do to restore it. It is a gift from your Heavenly Father. Accept it and run into His loving arms, that are wide open, waiting to embrace you!

I once heard Beth Moore say at a conference: "If you never perform a single wonder, you are the wonder—if you walk with God. It makes you a hero to your descendants."

What is keeping you from truly accepting God's love for you? Could there be unforgiveness in your heart or shame that you need to be free of? Both of these will impact your ability to accept God's love for you. Ask Him to reveal any areas that are holding you back from accepting His love.

Do you struggle to talk to God or to ask Him for anything because you feel you are not worthy? If so, surrender that to Him now. Start small. Ask for forgiveness. You can gradually increase your conversation, but your prayers do not need to be a certain length or with certain words, just talk to Him in your own words, as few or many as you like.

Journal any additional messages, thoughts, or ideas that God has placed on your heart:

Prayer Circles

Based on your revelations and reflections, what obstacles can you circle in prayer?

Details: Details:

Bible Verse: Bible Verse:

Transformational Tip #3: Keep Spiritual Snacks Handy

This is a great tip that I heard from a Joyce Meyer teaching. As she said, we always make sure that we have snacks handy to feed our body, so why wouldn't we make sure we have snacks available to feed our spirit.[8]

There are many ways this can be done. You can write Scripture on mirrors, put little booklets in your bag, car or pocket, or write verses on index cards and carry them with you. You can put Scripture on your walls, or have décor with your favorite verses on them.

We are blessed with technology that gives us easy access to all kinds of resources. You can download free Bible apps such as YouVersion on your phone so that it is always with you and available. Within YouVersion there are even several translations available in audio so you can listen to the Bible while you are driving or when you go for a walk.

There are numerous podcasts from a plethora of amazing preachers and Bible teachers that are all available via various devices such as smartphones or Apple TV, in addition to TV shows (even entire channels and networks), YouTube, DVD's, CD's, USB memory sticks and likely several other formats I am forgetting or don't even know about.

We have access to more resources than we could possibly read, watch, or listen to in our lifetime. We just need to tap into them and include them in our schedule. Commuting to and from work or school provides a great opportunity to listen to or watch (only if you are not driving—of course) these resources.

If you don't know where to start, ask your pastor or somebody you trust that is a mature Christ follower and has sound knowledge of the Bible. There are false teachers in the world, the Bible warns us about them, so you need to be sure that the teaching you are listening to aligns with the entirety of God's Word.

These "spiritual snacks" are crucial to feed your spirit and get the truth, which is God's Word, planted deep in your heart. They will help you come to truly know Jesus and have an intimate relationship with Him.

What is one thing that you will do to ensure you are feeding yourself spiritual snacks continuously?

Love—Day 6

Psalm 103 tells us that God's love for us is as high as the heavens, and although our life is like grass that is blown away in the wind and remembered no more, God's love is forever—from everlasting to everlasting!

This is important to remember when you find yourself getting your sense of worth from the things of this world (people, material possessions, titles, status, awards, achievements, recognition, etc.). Your life is like grass that is blown away in the wind and remembered no more; it is a mist that appears for a little while and then vanishes (James 4:14).

This does not mean that your life is not important. On the contrary: it means it is extremely important. *Eternally* important!

In 2 Corinthians 4:18, the apostle Paul tells us to "fix our eyes not on what is seen, but on what is unseen, since what is seen is temporary, but what is unseen is eternal."

It means you need to realize how important you are, how critical your time on earth is, and the incredible value that you have. You were chosen and called by God to display His splendor!

> Before I was born the LORD called me; from my mother's womb he has spoken my name. He made my mouth like a sharpened sword, in the shadow of his hand he hid me; he made me into a polished arrow and concealed me in his quiver. He said to me, "You are my servant, Israel, in whom I will display my splendor." (Isaiah 49:1–3)

Is there something temporary that you are striving to get your sense of worth from?

What do you expect to happen when you get what you have been striving for? How do you expect to feel?

What might you do differently when you have your eyes fixed on what is unseen, Jesus, instead of what is seen? How does an eternal perspective change the way you feel about what you have been striving for?

Journal any additional messages, thoughts, or ideas that God has placed on your heart:

Prayer Circles

Based on your revelations and reflections, what can you circle in prayer?

Details: Details:

Bible Verse: Bible Verse:

Transformational Tip #4: Choose a Focus Word

It is likely safe to say that we are all familiar with the principle that what we focus on grows. You may have heard it stated using different words, but I'm sure we have all experienced this principle in our lives. When we focus on a problem, all we see is the problem and it is difficult to see any solutions because the problem seems so big and appears to keep getting bigger. When we focus on the negative, the positive seems elusive—and vice versa—when we focus on the positive, the negative does not appear so big. We see this principle when gardening; if we neglect the flowers they do not grow as well as they do when we give them our attention and care. Or when trying to grow a business; it won't flourish by ignoring it and just hoping and praying for God's favor on it. It is the same with getting to know Jesus! It is not good enough to just want to know Him better—you actually have to take the steps towards knowing Him better! Knowing Him needs to become your focus.

A good way to do this is to determine an area in which you want to grow in your relationship with Jesus, and make that your focus for the year (if you find a year too long, try six months or even three months). Choose a word that defines that area of focus and make it your "focus word." Pick a theme verse to go along with your word. Then, for the entire period of time you have chosen, seek and study scriptures related to this word. Incorporate this area of focus into your prayer life, listen to messages, read books and do Bible studies that are all centered around your focus word.

If you struggle to believe God's love for you, choose "love" as your word of focus. Then, as mentioned above, seek and study God's Word completely focused on His love for you, not your love for Him. Even if you have accepted God's love for you, I recommend completing the exercise below as you can never remind yourself enough of His incredible, unfailing love for you.

Find a theme verse that expresses God's love for you and memorize it. Write it on your mirror, or create an index card to carry with you, or use YouVersion to create a picture of your verse with a beautiful background and then save it as the wallpaper on your phone or other devices. Or, record it in your phone so that you have it available to listen to.

Love—Day 7

God loves you so much that He pursues you even when you are not pursuing Him. His love found your soul worth dying for! He loves you uniquely, for the things that make you uniquely you. He delights in you, He believes in you and He is cheering for you. He understands you completely and loves you perfectly.

You can trust Him because He loves you SO much! He sacrificed everything for *you*! He was willing to die so that you can live in freedom. He cherishes you and wants nothing but the best for you.

His love has an eternal grip on you! You can count on His love; nothing can shake it. It is unfailing and lasts forever, from everlasting to everlasting.

> This is love: not that we loved God, but that he loved us and sent his Son as an atoning sacrifice for our sins. (1 John 4:10)

> I have loved you with an everlasting love; I have drawn you with unfailing kindness. (Jeremiah 31:3)

> "Though the mountains be shaken and the hills be removed, yet my unfailing love for you will not be shaken nor my covenant of peace be removed," says the LORD, who has compassion on you. (Isaiah 54:10)

I encourage you to dive into His everlasting arms today!

Find a place to rest in stillness and say out loud: "Jesus loves me. I can trust Him because He loves me so much." Let this sink in. Repeat this multiple times until you feel it permeating your soul. From this day forward, start each day with this exercise. When you open your eyes in the morning take thirty seconds to repeat these words and let that thought begin your day.

How do you think your life will be different when you truly grasp the depth of God's love for you?

Journal any additional messages, thoughts, or ideas that God has placed on your heart:

Prayer Circles

What thoughts, questions, or doubts about God's love can you circle in prayer?

Details: Details:

Bible Verse: Bible Verse:

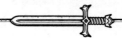

Transformational Tip #5: Journal

Journaling has multiple benefits. It is a great way to help you reflect deeper on what you are learning from God. Often God will provide additional insight through journaling.

After hearing a message at church, on a podcast, or at a conference, meditate (murmur over and over) on the message; journal the key points that spoke to you. If we don't do this, then the message is quickly forgotten: It is like the seeds, in the Parable of the Sower, that the birds come and snatch away before they can germinate and take root (Matthew 13:4). Take notes while listening to a message so that you have them to refer to later as you meditate on it further.

When praying, or reading the Bible, journal the highlights: Were there any messages God gave you specifically? Any key points that stood out or that you have questions about? Also, keep a praise journal where you capture all your answered prayers as well as things that you are grateful to God for, both big things and small things. Looking back at blessings and answered prayers are a great reminder of God's love for you, especially during seasons where you have trouble seeing the blessings and your prayers seem unanswered.

Another benefit of journaling is that it preserves what you have learned so that it can be used to help others. God will use every trial that you face and every obstacle that you overcome to help others that are battling similar trials and obstacles. Somebody else's freedom is on the other side of your struggle. Romans 8:28 tells us that God works all things for the good of those who love Him and are called according to His purpose. He will not waste your pain or your struggle—He will use it for good.

Hopefully *Sharpen Your Sword* is helping you with the practice of journaling. If you have not been completing the journaling exercise so far, what has been holding you back?

If you are journaling, what difference has it made in your faith journey? Is there anything you want to adjust to make it more effective?

If you are still having difficulty journaling, try using a different style. If you were writing out complete sentences, try writing a few key words or using bullet points; or maybe drawing a picture or using word art.

Practice journaling by writing down a struggle or trial that you are currently facing or have overcome. Capture the learnings that you can share with others who are in a similar situation.

Love—Day 8

God's love for us is *truth*. But we have a very real enemy. In John 10:10, Jesus tells us that Satan, who He calls "the thief," comes only to steal, kill and destroy—whereas, He has come to give us abundant life.

Colossians 2:15 tells us that Satan is already defeated; he was defeated by the cross; he has been disarmed and has no power. The only thing that he can do is plant thoughts in our mind and make us our own enemy. Jesus tells us that Satan is the father of lies (John 8:44). That is all he does, Satan is a liar.

He will plant lies in your mind: I am stupid, I am a failure, I am hopeless, I am unlovable, I am worthless, I have no purpose, I am _____.

You need to have on the full armor of God (Ephesians 6:10–17) so you can take those thoughts captive. You need to have on your shield of faith, your helmet of salvation, your belt of truth, your shoes of peace, your breastplate of righteousness, and your sword of the Spirit, which is the Word of God. This will prepare you for battle! Then the next time these lies come into your mind you can say:

NO—get behind me Satan!

I am chosen (1 Peter 2:9, Colossians 3:12).

I am a child of the one true King (Galatians 3:26, 1 Timothy 6:15).

I am the head and not the tail, I am above and not below (Deuteronomy 28:13).

I am fearfully and wonderfully made (Psalm 139:14), and I *will* fulfill the plan and purpose God has for me because by the blood of Jesus Christ, I AM A VICTOR!

As a Christ follower, you are a victor, and you don't want to negate what Jesus did for you on the cross by living in defeat.

Accepting God's profound love for you is fundamental to be fully suited with the armor of God. It is essentially the armor support system that holds all the pieces of the armor in place and gives it strength and stability, ensuring full protection.

What piece of your armor do you think might be missing or weakened?

How will embracing God's love for you change that?

Journal any additional messages, thoughts, or ideas that God has placed on your heart:

Prayer Circles

Choose two lies that you are fighting against and replace them with the truth of God's Word. Circle these truths in prayer.

Details: Details:

Bible Verse: Bible Verse:

Love—Day 9

Would you find it easier to believe that a stranger you just met loves you or that a family member or friend that you know really well loves you? I think it would be safe to say that we would all answer this with the latter. Why would you expect it to be any different with Jesus? How can you believe He loves you if you don't really know Him?

Let's look back at our theme verse:

> And I pray that you, being rooted and established in love, may have power, together with all the Lord's holy people, to grasp how wide and long and high and deep is the love of Christ, and to **know** this love that surpasses knowledge—that you may be filled to the measure of all the fullness of God. (Ephesians 3:17–19, emphasis mine)

The Greek word for *know* in this verse is the word "ginosko" (gē-nō'-skō).[9] There are a few different Greek words used in the Bible for *know*. They each have slightly different meanings or mean different levels of knowledge. This particular word means a relational or experiential knowledge rather than an intellectual knowledge; it is referring to having a personal relationship with Jesus. Often, we have knowledge of Jesus in our head, but we don't *know* Him in our heart. We know *of* Him and we know *about* Him but we don't actually *know* Him.

The only way to truly get to know Him is to spend time with Him. You can't know Jesus from a distance. You need to have a relationship with Him. You need to experience Him in a close and personal way.

Do you *ginosko* Jesus? Do you *ginosko* His love that surpasses knowledge?

Apostle John referred to himself as the one that Jesus loved. Do you feel confident in saying that about yourself?

Spend some extra time in prayer today. Ask God to show you something that you don't know about Him.

Journal what God revealed to you about Himself or any additional messages, thoughts, or ideas that God has placed on your heart:

Prayer Circles

Based on your revelations, reflections, thoughts, and ideas, what or whom can you circle in prayer?

Details: Details:

Bible Verse: Bible Verse:

Love—Day 10 (Conclusion)

Psalm 136 is a psalm of gratitude and praise to our Almighty God. It is traditionally sung at the end of the Jewish Passover meal and was probably prayed or sung at the Last Supper with Jesus.[10] Jesus would have been reminded twenty-six times that God's love endures forever before He went to the cross. It repeats over and over that His faithful love lasts forever, emphasizing the importance of understanding His never-failing love for you. When you read this psalm, do not skip over those important words because they are repetitive. Instead, allow the magnitude of their meaning to sink deeper into your heart each time you say them. This psalm captures the essence of the all-encompassing love of your all-powerful Creator. It is a reminder of the One who reigns over everything, who created the heavens and the earth in all its beauty for you to enjoy, who rescues you from your enemies, frees you from your captors, protects you from your adversaries, brings justice to your oppressors, and provides your every need; the one and only true God who loves *you* completely, uniquely, faithfully, and unfailingly forever and ever.

Let your heart overflow with praise to the Eternal, for He is good,
 for His faithful love lasts forever.
Praise the True God *who reigns* over all other gods,
 for His faithful love lasts forever.
Praise the Lord *who reigns* over all other lords,
 for His faithful love lasts forever.
To Him who alone does marvelous wonders,
 for His faithful love lasts forever.
Who created the heavens with skill *and artistry*,
 for His faithful love lasts forever.
Who laid out dry land over the waters,
 for His faithful love lasts forever.
Who made the great *heavenly* lights,
 for His faithful love lasts forever.
The sun to reign by day,
 for His faithful love lasts forever.
The moon and stars to reign by night,
 for His faithful love lasts forever.
To Him who struck down the firstborn of the Egyptians,
 for His faithful love lasts forever.

Who set Israel free from Egyptian masters,
 for His faithful love lasts forever.
With *fierce strength*, a mighty hand, and an outstretched arm,
 for His faithful love lasts forever.
To Him who split the Red Sea in two *and made a path between the divided waters*,
 for His faithful love lasts forever.
Then allowed Israel to pass *safely* through *on dry ground*,
 for His faithful love lasts forever.
To Him who crushed Pharaoh and his army in *the waters of* the Red Sea,
 for His faithful love lasts forever.
Who guided His people through the desert,
 for His faithful love lasts forever.
Who struck down mighty kings,
 for His faithful love lasts forever.
Who slaughtered famous kings,
 for His faithful love lasts forever.
Sihon, the king of the Amorites,
 for His faithful love lasts forever.
And Og, the king of Bashan,
 for His faithful love lasts forever.

To Him who gave the conquered land as an inheritance,
    for His faithful love lasts forever.
Who made the land a heritage to Israel, His servant,
    for His faithful love lasts forever.
To Him who remembered us when we were nearly defeated,
    for His faithful love lasts forever.

Who rescued us from our enemies,
    for His faithful love lasts forever.
Who provides food for every living thing,
    for His faithful love lasts forever.
Let your heart overflow with praise to the True God of heaven,
    for His faithful love lasts forever.
(Psalm 136 The Voice, bolded emphasis mine)

Receive His faithful never-ending love today. Open your heart to this precious gift. Like a parent loves a newborn unconditionally without the baby needing to do anything for them in return, even greater is your Heavenly Father's love for you. He doesn't love you for what you can do for Him, He loves you because you are His child. You are the one that Jesus loves.

Confidently exclaim that truth. Declare it boldly: **"I am the one that Jesus loves!"**

Journal any concluding thoughts that God has placed on your heart regarding His love for you:

Prayer Circles

Based on your concluding thoughts, whom or what can you circle in prayer? Perhaps one circle can be a prayer of thanksgiving.

Details: Details:

Bible Verse: Bible Verse:

TRUST

Trusting God

I was at an awkward stage in my life when my daughter, who is now an adult, and I were having difficulty determining my role as a parent. There is always that question of when do I get involved and when do I let go and let God? I did not become a Christ-follower until my daughter was fifteen, so I feel like I have had this question for most of my Christian life. It took me a while to start asking this as I did not bring my faith into my parenting right away. I did not intentionally exclude it; it was strictly an oversight on my part and part of my learning process. My point being, when children are younger, your role as a parent is clearer because of their complete dependence on you. As my daughter went from a teenager to an adult, I knew I needed to let go and let her have her own journey of faith.

During this process, I had many conversations with God, and in one of them I asked Him why I trusted Him with myself but didn't have the same level of trust in Him with my daughter. I was not expecting the answer I received back. He told me that it wasn't that I trusted Him with myself and not with my daughter, it was that I didn't trust Him at all!

He continued to reveal to me that what I was actually trusting was what was in my ability to control. I could control my obedience to God but I could not control my daughter's obedience to God (or anybody else's for that matter). In reality, I was putting my trust in myself—not God!

So I had to ask myself: "Do I trust God, really?" This section of the devotional study is a result of the trust journey that God took me on to answer this question. We will unpack what it means to trust God, identify any areas where we are not trusting God, set some expectations that will help us navigate the unknown, and explore some suggestions that can help build our trust in God. Many of the thoughts and ideas in this section came from learnings I received through the *Jesus Calling* devotional written by Sarah Young. This is a great devotional that I would highly recommend!

> Trust in the LORD with all your heart and lean not on your own understanding; in all your ways acknowledge him, and he will make your paths straight. (Proverbs 3:5–6)

Trust—Day 1

So what does trust actually mean? One of the Hebrew words for *trust* in the Bible is "batach" (bä·takh'). This means, "to have confidence, to be secure, to be bold, hope."[11] The dictionary goes on to define *trust* in this manner: "to rely or depend on; to believe; confident expectation of something; to commit to the care of; and to be confident of something present or future."[12]

These are all such powerful definitions. There is nothing I want more than to have confidence in God and to have that reassuring feeling of security. We all long for someone that we can depend on. Too often we put our dependence on people, but it is only God who will never let us down. Everything of this world is temporary and, because of the Fall (Genesis 3), we as humans are flawed. There was only one perfect person and that was Jesus. Nobody else will ever be perfect; we must stop expecting them to be. This does not mean that you can never trust anybody or have deep, meaningful relationships with people. God made us for relationship and we can trust one another, it just won't be to the same level. Only God can fulfill the depth and entirety of the definition of trust. Only He can embody its true meaning. We will make mistakes, we will offer incorrect advice, we will not be available all the time, we will not always be able to meet a specific need. Only God can meet every need, offer perfect advice all the time, and be there 100% of the time we need Him. Our trust in people is restrained by the effects of the Fall. Our trust in God is completely unrestrained! It has no limits! We can completely commit our life to the care of God without the fear of being let down. We can be confident in our expectations, not only for now but also for the future. We can be bold and believe; knowing that God is taking care of us. Even when our situation looks hopeless, we can have hope. That is trust.

Which of the definitions listed means the most to you? Why?

Can you think of a time when you put your trust in a person instead of putting it in God? What was the result? How would the result or the process of getting to the result have been different if you had put your trust in God instead?

Journal any additional messages, thoughts, or ideas that God has placed on your heart:

Prayer Circles

Based on your revelations, reflections, thoughts, and ideas, what or whom can you circle in prayer?

Details: Details:

Bible Verse: Bible Verse:

Trust—Day 2

Now we know what trust means, but what does it truly look like? How do we know whether or not we are really trusting God? The following verses from the Bible provide great indicators to answer these questions (emphasis mine):

> May the God of hope fill you with all **joy** and **peace** as you trust in him, so that you may overflow with **hope** by the power of the Holy Spirit. (Romans 15:13)

> You will keep *him* in **perfect peace**, *Whose* mind *is* stayed *on You,* Because he trusts in You. (Isaiah 26:3 NKJV)

> Surely God is my salvation; I will trust and **not be afraid**. The LORD, the LORD himself, is **my strength** and **my defense**; he has become my salvation. (Isaiah 12:2)

> When I am afraid, I put my trust in you. In God, whose word I praise—in God I trust and am **not afraid**. What can mere mortals do to me? (Psalm 56:3–4)

> I trust in you; do not let me be put to shame, nor let my enemies triumph over me. **No** one who hopes in you will ever be put to **shame**, but shame will come on those who are treacherous without cause. (Psalm 25:2–3)

> Bring **joy** to your servant, Lord, for I put my trust in you. (Psalm 86:4)

As shown in the verses above, when we trust in the Lord we will have hope, joy, and peace. We will have strength and no fear. And we will have no shame. Conversely, when we do not trust Him, the opposite will be true. We will be anxious and fearful. Our hearts will not be at peace.

What are the areas in your life where you do not have peace, joy, or hope? What do you worry about? What are your fears?

Is there something in your life that makes you feel shameful? Is there an area in your life where you feel weak or defenseless?

Sometimes these areas may not be obvious to us. You may need to pray for God to reveal any areas where you do not trust Him. Psalm 139:23 says "Search me, God, and know my heart; test me and know my anxious thoughts." This verse may be one of your prayer circles today.

Journal any additional messages, thoughts, or ideas that God has placed on your heart:

Prayer Circles

What area in your life, that requires growth in your trust in God, can you circle in prayer?

Details: Details:

Bible Verse: Bible Verse:

Transformational Tip #1: Have a Teachable Spirit, be Willing to be Changed

It is important to have an open mind and an open heart so you can be receptive to what God has to teach you, even when it is difficult to hear.

> Do not conform to the pattern of this world, but be transformed
> by the renewing of your mind. (Romans 12:2)

Joshua had a teachable spirit. He served eagerly under Moses for forty years. Joshua was with Moses when he met face to face with God in the Tent of Meeting, and when Moses returned to the camp, Joshua stayed in the tent (Exodus 33:11). He was hungry for the presence of God! His open mind and open heart prepared him to confidently receive and carry out the inconceivable battle plan that God laid out years later in order to conquer Jericho (read Joshua 6 on the Fall of Jericho). It would have taken huge confidence and trust in the Lord and amazing humility to follow those orders! Let's face it, most of us would be too embarrassed to instruct the army we are leading to march around the city until we tell them to stop, and then to yell when we tell them to yell. We would be too concerned about what they would think of us, too scared that our leadership skills would be laughed at. Then our mind would likely start to question if this really came from God, trying to justify reasons not to follow these strange, illogical instructions.

But Joshua did not question God or worry about what people would think. He did not conform to the pattern of the world because his mind had been renewed by willingly receiving all that God was teaching him.

Open your heart and mind to receive what God is teaching you through His Word, prayer, and through the spiritual leaders that He has placed in your life.

Take some time to think of the faith-filled, Christ-centered mentors, teachers, preachers, friends, and leaders that God has blessed you with. Pray a prayer of thanksgiving for these people. If you don't currently have any, pray for God to direct you to some.

> Trust in the LORD with *all* your heart and lean not on your own understanding; in *all* your ways acknowledge him, and he will make your paths straight. (Proverbs 3:5–6, emphasis mine)

The verses above provide additional insight into what it means to trust God. It tells us to trust with *all* our heart. When I looked up this Hebrew word for *all* (kol), it means exactly that: "all, everything, the whole."[13] Anything less than 100% is not trust.

We can't trust God with some things but not with others. We either trust Him or we don't. We trust who He is, His Word, and His promises or we don't. Trust is not conditional. Trust is not partial.

I read a great book written by John Bevere called *Good or God* that tells a story that demonstrates this well. The story is about a man and a woman who are dating. The man has fallen completely in love with the woman. She is everything he has been looking for in a wife. So he decides he is going to propose and he plans a very romantic date to carry out the proposal. On the night of the date, everything is going great and he finds the perfect opportunity to pop the question. He gets down on his knee and asks her to be his wife. She is so excited and immediately accepts the proposal and claims that she is going to be the best wife ever for him. Then she pauses and says, "There is just one thing though, I have some other boyfriends that I would still like to see once in a while." The man is stunned and can't believe what he is hearing. He thinks she must be joking. (Just a quick aside, this would be an absolutely terrible time for a joke of this nature; I would advise against it). But she isn't, so he adamantly replies: "No, that is not acceptable. That will not work." She really loves him and does want to be his wife so she decides to modify her request slightly to see if that will change his mind. She says, "Well, how about if I see my other boyfriends just one day of the year. For 364 days I will be completely committed to you and will be the best wife you have ever seen, but one day of the year I get to see my other boyfriends." Of course, he did not agree with this. So she continued to negotiate; she tried for four hours and when that was unsuccessful she asked for just twenty minutes a year with her other boyfriends. Needless to say, the man was heartbroken and decided to end the relationship altogether. Nothing less than 100% commitment would do.[14]

This is a perfect picture of Jesus and the church. The Bible tells us that Jesus is the bridegroom and that we, as believers, otherwise known as the church, are His bride. He expects the same thing from us—nothing less than 100% of our commitment and our trust.

Read Luke 18:18–30.

What are you hanging on to that you have not yet surrendered to Jesus? Is there an area that you feel you still need to keep within your own control?

What is it that would make you sad if Jesus told you that you had to give it up?

Journal any additional messages, thoughts, or ideas that God has placed on your heart:

Prayer Circles

Based on your revelations, reflections, thoughts, and ideas, what or whom can you circle in prayer?

Details: Details:

Bible Verse: Bible Verse:

Transformational Tip #2: Don't Skimp on the Time you Spend with Jesus

Read the story of Mary and Martha in Luke 10:38–42.

I think most of us relate very closely to Martha. We have a to-do list that *needs* to get done. It certainly cannot be acceptable to sit down and spend quiet time in God's Word if there are dirty dishes in the sink or yard work to be done. We even use the excuse: "Well I wouldn't be able to focus anyway when I have so much to do. I just need to finish these chores first and then I will sit down and spend time praying and reading my Bible." But one task leads to the next and then it is time to go to work, make a meal, pick up kids, take the kids to their activities, clean up one last mess and before you know it you are exhausted and needing to go to bed. So tomorrow, for sure, you will spend time in the Word. Morning comes, but you are still exhausted from the day before and you are not much of a morning person so you likely wouldn't retain anything if you did it now anyways, but for sure you will make some time later in the day. And the cycle repeats.

We need to stop and remember what Jesus said to Martha: "Mary has chosen what is better, and it will not be taken away from her." Mary chose to sit at the feet of Jesus, to listen to His teaching, to get to know Him. When it comes time to give an account of your life, it won't be how much money you earned, how great you were at sports, how tidy your house was, or how many activities you had your kids in that will be discussed. Jesus tells us in Matthew 7:21–23 that not everybody who calls Him "Lord" will enter the kingdom of heaven because He never knew them. Jesus wants you to *know* Him. When you include God in every part of your day, your priorities become clear and you get more done in a day. Seek, then schedule. Martin Luther once said, "I have so much to do that I shall have to spend the first three hours in prayer."

Time with Jesus pleases Him; He delights in it! And, it strengthens and equips you for the moment, the day, the week, the month, and the season ahead. Like any relationship, the more time you spend with someone, the more you know them, and the more you trust them. To trust Jesus, you need to know Him!

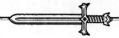

Do you include Jesus in every part of your life? Do you have a quiet time set aside every day to spend reading and meditating on His Word?

Do you let your schedule determine your time with God rather than letting God help you determine your schedule?

What will you adjust to make spending time with Jesus a priority?

Trust—Day 4

> "For I know the plans I have for you," declares the LORD, "plans to prosper you and not to harm you, plans to give you hope and a future." (Jeremiah 29:11)

God knows His plans for us. But we don't. I believe that almost all our fears stem from the unknown. We get anxious when we don't know what is going to happen. We think that if we only knew what would happen, regardless of the outcome—good or bad—then we can be prepared for it.

But 2 Corinthians 5:7 in the New King James Version tells us that "we walk by faith, not by sight."

There are known realities that will help you to navigate the unknown. We will examine five expectations that you can set that will help prepare you to walk by faith.

1. **Expect God's timing to be different than yours**

    It is important to realize that time is a trainer and you need to embrace the growth that you experience in the waiting. One of the ways that God asserts His sovereignty is in His timing.

    > Wait for the LORD; be strong and take heart and wait for the LORD. (Psalm 27:14)

    We must remember that we only see a tiny, minute speck of the big picture but Jesus sees it all, from beginning to end; He makes His decisions based on ALL the information, whereas we are trying to make decisions based on MISSING information.

    Jesus has no limits! Ephesians 3:20 tells us that "[He] is able to do immeasurably more than all we ask or imagine."

    Let Him set the pace; slow down and enjoy the journey!

What unanswered prayers do you have that you may have given up on, or that you are wondering if they will ever be answered?

Reflect on either an existing unanswered prayer or a prayer that took a long time to be answered. What did you learn during the waiting? Is there an area of growth that you now recognize would not have occurred if you had not experienced that time of waiting?

Journal any additional messages, thoughts, or ideas that God has placed on your heart:

Prayer Circles

Based on your reflections, what or whom can you circle in prayer?

Details:

Details:

Bible Verse:

Bible Verse:

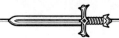

Transformational Tip #3: Make "I Trust You, Jesus" Your New Slogan

We have learned that fear, worry, anxiety, shame, or a lack of peace, joy, or hope are all indicators that we are not trusting the Lord. At the first sign of any of these attributes, stop what you are doing and say "I trust You, Jesus." Repeat it over and over if you have to. As soon as your thoughts start to lead you down a path that causes you to have any of these feelings, interrupt the thought with "I trust You, Jesus." Continue to say it until your thoughts are no longer directed down that path of destruction, until your thoughts are taken captive to be obedient to Christ.

> We demolish arguments and every pretension that sets itself up against the knowledge of God, and we take captive every thought to make it obedient to Christ. (2 Corinthians 10:5)

Sometimes we may be in the heat of the moment where even "I trust You, Jesus" is too long to get out. In those moments, whisper His name, "Jesus," to redirect your thoughts and keep your focus on Him. There is power in the name of Jesus! It is the name above any other name! It is by this name alone, the name of Jesus, that we have eternal life!

> Therefore God exalted him to the highest place and gave him the name that is above every name, that at the name of Jesus every knee should bow, in heaven and on earth and under the earth, and every tongue acknowledge that Jesus Christ is Lord, to the glory of God the Father. (Philippians 2:9–11)

> I write these things to you who believe in the name of the Son of God so that you may know that you have eternal life. (1 John 5:13)

Practice this habit for a week and journal the results. Be specific enough about the situation and the feelings you were experiencing to act as a good reminder when you refer to it later. Journaling the results will provide a good point of reference that can encourage you to continue with this habit of saying "I trust You, Jesus" so it becomes a natural response when needed.

2. **Expect obstacles**

In John 16:33, Jesus tells us that in this world we *will* have trouble. He doesn't say *if* we have trouble—He says we will. But, He also tells us to take heart, because He has overcome the world.

> God is our refuge and strength, an *ever-present* help in trouble. (Psalm 46:1, emphasis mine)

We don't need to fear when we have troubles, Jesus is our Helper to overcome all obstacles. His grace is sufficient for us, for His power is made perfect in weakness. The apostle Paul goes on to tell us:

> Therefore I will boast all the more gladly about my weaknesses, so that Christ's power may rest on me. That is why, for Christ's sake, I delight in weaknesses, in insults, in hardships, in persecutions, in difficulties. For when I am weak, then I am strong. (2 Corinthians 12:9–10)

We can take comfort knowing that we can rely on Christ's strength in our time of need; that He is an *ever-present help* in our time of trouble.

Jesus gave us victory; no matter what trouble we are facing, we are already victorious through the crucifixion and resurrection of Jesus Christ! We attain this victorious life by living in deep dependence on Him; by keeping an eternal perspective.

What obstacles are you currently facing that you have not been depending on the resurrection power of Jesus Christ to help you overcome?

Are you trying to control the outcome? Or, have you surrendered it to God and trust that the outcome will be *the best* no matter what it is?

Journal any additional messages, thoughts, or ideas that God has placed on your heart:

Prayer Circles

Based on your revelations and reflections, what obstacles can you circle in prayer?

Details: Details:

Bible Verse: Bible Verse:

Trust—Day 6

Yesterday we celebrated the victory that Jesus has given us on the cross. However, victory does not equal success; which brings us to the next point:

3. **Expect many failures**

    As part of our worldly tendencies, we most often view failure from a negative perspective. We reflect and fret over everything that went wrong, neglecting to recognize what we have learned in the process.

    It is important to realize that failure equals growth. Each failure is followed by a growth spurt and increases your dependence on Jesus. You must persevere!

    > Let perseverance finish its work so that you may be mature and complete, not lacking anything. (James 1:4)

    Regardless of the obstacles you face or the failures you experience, each time you confirm your trust in Jesus you are making a deposit in His treasury; the interest compounds continuously, storing up a treasure of trust and peace. And the more you trust Him, the more He empowers you to trust Him.

    > But store up for yourselves treasures in heaven…For where your treasure is, there your heart will be also. (Matthew 6:20–21)

    I had always thought of these verses in terms of finances and possessions, but I love them in this context: that my treasure is trust and peace and that is what will be in my heart.

    However, just like money, we need to save up so that it is available when we need it.

    Practice trusting in quiet times so that you will be prepared when the storms come; so that you will have a treasury of peace to draw from regardless of the circumstances surrounding you.

What aspects of your life have you considered a failure? Look back on these areas and identify any growth that occurred because of the failure. This can be spiritual growth, character growth, physical or emotional strength, wisdom that was gained, etc.

How has the growth that was identified helped you in other areas of life? (i.e. Helped you overcome other obstacles or achieve something you couldn't have achieved without this growth, or allowed you to use your testimony to help others.)

Journal any additional messages, thoughts, or ideas that God has placed on your heart:

Prayer Circles

Based on your revelations, reflections, thoughts, and ideas, what or whom can you circle in prayer?

Details: Details:

Bible Verse: Bible Verse:

Transformational Tip #4: Praise Him and Thank Him

The Bible tells us that God inhabits (dwells, abides, is enthroned on) the praises of His people.

> Yet you are holy, enthroned on the praises of Israel. (Psalm 22:3 ESV)

There are two kinds of praise that we offer to God: a spontaneous overflow of joy, or a disciplined act of will. He dwells **equally** in both. Although it may feel fake to you when you are praising Him out of a forced act of discipline, He sees your sacrifice to praise and thank Him when nothing in you feels like doing so.

When you thank Him in all situations you show your trust in His sovereignty. Living in an attitude and discipline of praise and thankfulness will help you to live in the closeness of His presence. It brings intimacy and peace.

> Rejoice in the Lord always. I will say it again: Rejoice! Let your gentleness be evident to all. The Lord is near. Do not be anxious about anything, but in every situation, by prayer and petition, with thanksgiving, present your requests to God. And the peace of God, which transcends all understanding, will guard your hearts and your minds in Christ Jesus. (Philippians 4:4–7)

Rejoice, the Lord is near, do not be anxious, pray with gratitude, and you will have peace that transcends understanding!

One of the things we tend to do when we have unanswered prayers is to make the same requests, the same petitions, over and over again. Instead, pray prayers of thanksgiving for the answers that are coming. This does two things: first, it increases your faith and trust. When you are thanking God, belief is ignited within your body, soul, and spirit that those promises are being received. Secondly, prayers of thanksgiving will diffuse tension and invite peace into your heart. If you keep restating your concerns then you are living in a constant state of tension, always focused on the problem. Prayers of thanksgiving keep your focus on His presence and His promises—it totally changes your perspective!

Is there something in your life right now that has been keeping you from praising God? An area that requires a disciplined act of will to praise Him? If so, acknowledge it and commit to finding at least one thing to praise God for. It may be a beautiful sunrise or sunset, the beauty and majesty of Creation, a warm blanket, a soft pillow, family, friends, or a hot bowl of soup. Start small, and don't stop if it feels fake. Remember, He sees your sacrifice!

4. **Expect surprises**

Every day with Jesus is an adventure!

Jesus is your GPS for each day, equipping you for the journey ahead. Only He knows the destination. Unlike a regular roadmap, don't search for the easiest and quickest route—be willing to follow wherever He leads. Regardless of where the path may lead or what it might look like, with steep inclines or sharp drop offs, the safest place to be is by His side.

Each day is a priceless, one-of-a-kind gift that cannot be repeated—relinquish control, let go, and enjoy it to the fullest!

> This is the day that the LORD has made; let us rejoice and be glad in it. (Psalm 118:24 ESV)

When you follow Jesus, your life will never be boring or predictable! He always has a better plan than you could possibly imagine. Be careful to allow margin in your schedule for His surprises. Remember, He already has it all mapped out. Sometimes surprises might appear in the form of interruptions or inconveniences. Margin in your schedule provides a perspective shift, allowing you to recognize these subtle surprises as opportunities rather than inconveniences.

> *Instead,* You direct me on the path that leads to *a beautiful* life. As I walk with You, the pleasures are never-ending, and I know true joy *and contentment.* (Psalm 16:11 The Voice)

What is the most recent surprise that Jesus has blessed you with?

Do you have margin in your schedule? If not, what steps can you take to add some in?

Journal any additional messages, thoughts, or ideas that God has placed on your heart:

Prayer Circles

Based on your revelations, reflections, thoughts, and ideas, what or whom can you circle in prayer?

Details: Details:

Bible Verse: Bible Verse:

5. **Expect God's Promises**

God has made *thousands* of promises to His people that are recorded in the Bible.

Scripture tells us that *all* those promises are fulfilled through Jesus Christ.

> For no matter how many promises God has made, they are "Yes" in Christ. And so through him the "Amen" is spoken by us to the glory of God. Now it is God who makes both us and you stand firm in Christ. He anointed us, set his seal of ownership on us, and put his Spirit in our hearts as a deposit, guaranteeing what is to come. (2 Corinthians 1:20–21)

God is light (1 John 1:5) and love (1 John 4:16); in Him there is no darkness. He wants nothing but the best for you. He is not looking to trick you. He wants to keep His promises to you.

Here are several of God's promises that He made to those who trust in Him:

Proverbs 3:5–6 – trust = **straight paths**
Nahum 1:7 – trust = **God's care**
Psalm 62:8 – trust = **refuge**
Proverbs 28:25 – trust = **prosperity**
Psalm 125:1 – trust = **unable to be shaken, endures forever**
Psalm 119:66 – trust = **knowledge and good judgment**
Psalm 13:5 – trust = **a heart that rejoices**
Psalm 22:4 – trust = **deliverance**
Psalm 25:2–3 – trust = **triumph over our enemies**
Psalm 37:3–4 – trust = **safety and the desires of our heart**
Psalm 40:4 – trust = **blessed**
Psalm 44:6–7 – trust = **victory**

And, of course, we can't forget the **perfect peace, joy** and **hope** that we will have, as stated in Isaiah 26:3 and Romans 15:13.

These are POWERFUL promises!

Pick two of the promises listed that speak the loudest to you in your current season. Look up these two verses, in your favorite translation, and use them to make your circles of prayer. Write the full verse in the space provided.

Journal any additional messages, thoughts, or ideas that God has placed on your heart:

Prayer Circles

Create your circles of prayer based on the two promises that you chose.

Details: Details:

Bible Verse: Bible Verse:

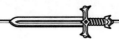

Transformational Tip #5: Remember His Promises

God's Word tells us that when we trust in the Lord we will have safety, deliverance, refuge, triumph over our enemies, prosperity, knowledge, good judgment, a heart that rejoices, and blessings.

Remembering these promises provides great incentive. I think we can all agree that when we know the reward at the end of the path, we are much more inclined to choose the right path.

Remembering is important. God had to remind the Israelites numerous times to remember how He brought them out of Egypt and freed them from slavery. And when Joshua led the Israelites across the Jordan, into the Promised Land, God had them take twelve stones from the riverbed to set up a memorial to the people of Israel to help them remember.

> In the future, when your children ask you, 'What do these stones mean?' tell them that the flow of the Jordan was cut off before the ark of the covenant of the LORD. When it crossed the Jordan, the waters of the Jordan were cut off. These stones are to be a memorial to the people of Israel forever. (Joshua 4:6–7)

As humans, we get distracted easily and it doesn't take us long to forget God's faithfulness and all that He has done for us. We develop spiritual amnesia very quickly! We tend to focus on what has not yet been done. Keeping God's promises at the forefront of your mind as a remembrance will deepen your trust in God.

Praise journals are a great way to capture God's faithfulness and keep it at the forefront of your mind. Have a separate journal where you record all your answered prayers, praise reports, and things you are thankful for. During the times when God seems to be silent, read through your praise journal to remind yourself that God is faithful and He keeps His promises.

Write out the verses listed in *Trust—Day 8* in a place where they will be handy for you to meditate on them regularly. You can write them on index cards and carry them with you; or, write them in your praise journal so you always know where to go to find them.

Pick one or two of the verses that are the most applicable to you at the moment and memorize them. Being able to recall the verse from memory is very powerful!

Trust—Day 9 (Conclusion)

So that's it. Easy, right? All we have to do is have a teachable spirit, spend lots of time with Jesus, accept His timing, tell Him repeatedly that we trust Him, praise Him and thank Him in every circumstance, and focus on His promises—then we will **never** fear, **never** worry, and we will **always** have peace when our prayers are not yet answered. It won't matter what obstacles we face or failures we experience—we will always trust Him. We will walk around filled with peace, joy, and hope **all the time**!

I don't know about you, but to me that seems impossible. And it is. We can't do it on our own. But, the good news is, we don't have to! Jesus gave us victory on the cross and we can do all things through Christ who gives us strength (Philippians 4:13). Nothing is impossible with God (Matthew 19:26)!

The only way we can surrender and trust completely is by the grace that He has saturated us with.

And even though we may have setbacks and moments of failure where we realize we are not trusting Him, or just new areas that require our trust (there will *always* be new areas that require our trust), Scripture tells us that there is nothing in all creation that is able to separate us from the love of God that is in Christ Jesus our Lord (Romans 8:39). And He who began a good work in us will carry it on to completion until the day of Christ Jesus (Philippians 1:6). That is GOOD NEWS!!

As you draw closer to Jesus, obey His commands, deposit your trust into His treasury, and relinquish control every day you *will* deepen your dependence on Him and you *will* be able to live with peace, joy, and hope in your hearts regardless of the circumstances around you.

My prayer for each of you is Romans 15:13: "May the God of hope fill you with all joy and peace as you trust in him, so that you may overflow with hope by the power of the Holy Spirit."

Journal any concluding messages, thoughts, or ideas that God has placed on your heart about trusting Him:

Prayer Circles

Based on your revelations, reflections, thoughts, and ideas, what or whom can you circle in prayer?

Details:

Details:

Bible Verse:

Bible Verse:

HUMILITY

Humility: The Nature of a Servant

I used to think that to be humble meant admitting that I was wrong. The thought of being humbled would stir up all kinds of negative emotions, it would make me feel exposed and vulnerable. In a world that teaches us that we need to be self-sufficient, self-confident, and independent— exposing our vulnerability is not highly regarded. If I admitted I was wrong, wouldn't that make me appear weak? Our society has taught us not to show our weaknesses, that we must be strong. But I think there is even more to these negative emotions than that. We can get a deeper understanding of our adverse feelings towards humility when we look at its antithesis, pride.

In *Mere Christianity,* C.S. Lewis describes pride like this, "There is one vice of which no man in the world is free; which every one in the world loathes when he sees it in someone else...There is no fault which makes a man more unpopular, and no fault which we are more unconscious of in ourselves. And the more we have it ourselves, the more we dislike it in others."[15]

To help us understand why pride is so ingrained in the core of humanity, let's look back to when pride first entered the world.

Pride is the root of all sin. It is pride that caused sin to enter the world (in fact, if we look back even farther it is pride that caused the devil to become the devil). Adam and Eve were surrounded by luxurious gardens that had everything they could possibly need. They even got to walk in the garden with God! They had all kinds of trees that were pleasing to the eye and good for food (Genesis 2:9). They only had one rule, just ONE: do not eat from the tree of the knowledge of good and evil. The tree of *life* was also in the garden and they were free to eat from that one. There was only one tree that God asked them not to eat from. But all it took was one suggestion—from a serpent, no less—that God was trying to keep something from them, to make them disobey God's one rule (see Genesis 2 and 3). Even though they were already made in the image of God, the serpent was able to plant doubt in their mind. The pride of wanting to be in control and to have more wisdom than what God had already provided (I'm thinking that God must have given them an abundance of intelligence for Adam to be able to name all the living creatures!), caused Eve to look at the tree of the knowledge of good and evil with lust in her eyes. It was pride that caused her to give in to her own selfish desires and disobey God's command.

We are all born with a sinful nature—we are all born with pride. Humility goes against our nature. And pride is rooted so deep within our nature that it is often difficult to recognize. It manifests in so many different ways that we don't even connect them all to pride. Our pride will even keep us from realizing we are prideful! It is something that is difficult to admit and humbling ourselves is one of the most challenging things to do.

Having a truly humble heart is impossible without Jesus Christ and the work of Holy Spirit within us! You can't be truly humble without knowing who you are in Christ. However, I found that in order to know who I am in Christ I needed to have some form of humility as a starting point. This appears to be paradoxical; a catch-22 of sorts. I think the paradox is resolved by looking at humility as a spectrum with worldly humility at one end and biblical humility at the other end. Finding your identity in Christ is the pivot point where worldly humility transitions to biblical humility. As we continue our journey through the sanctification process, the humility becomes purer.

This section is to help you develop self-awareness so you can recognize and acknowledge any prideful ways that are hindering your progress to the pivot point. It will help you remove prideful barriers so that God's love can sink into your heart and bring transformation out of which purified humility will flow.

As we move through this section of the devotional study, we will look at the importance that God has placed on humility and why. We will learn what it means to be humble, examine some expressions of humility that are shown in the Bible, look at a few examples of pride, and reflect on the promises that the Bible says we will receive when we have a humble heart.

When Jesus came, He was an example of how we are intended to live— the way Adam and Eve would have lived prior to letting pride enter the world.

Apostle Paul encourages us to imitate the humility that Jesus exampled. Meditate on these verses as you work through this section.

Therefore if you have any encouragement from being united with Christ, if any comfort from his love, if any common sharing in the Spirit, if any tenderness and compassion, then make my joy complete by being like-minded, having the same love, being one in spirit and of one mind. Do nothing out of selfish ambition or vain conceit. Rather, in humility value others above yourselves, not looking to your own interests but each of you to the interests of the others. In your relationships with one another, have the same mindset as Christ Jesus:

Who, being in very nature God,
    did not consider equality with God
    something to be used to his own advantage;
rather, he made himself nothing
    by taking the very nature of a servant,
    being made in human likeness.
And being found in appearance as a man,
    he humbled himself
    by becoming obedient to death—
    even death on a cross!
Therefore God exalted him to the highest place
    and gave him the name that is above every name,
that at the name of Jesus every knee should bow,
    in heaven and on earth and under the earth,
and every tongue acknowledge that Jesus Christ is Lord,
    to the glory of God the Father. (Philippians 2:1–11)

Humility—Day 1

Before we can discuss the importance of humility in our walk with Jesus, we need to have a base understanding of what it is. To do this, we need to look further than just the dictionary definition, as it does not give an accurate representation of the biblical meaning of humility.

The dictionary tells us that *humility* is "the quality or condition of being humble; modest opinion or estimate of one's own importance, rank, etc."[16] And when we look up *humble,* it means "not proud or arrogant; modest; courteously respectful; having a feeling of insignificance, inferiority, subservience; low in rank, importance, status, quality, etc.; to make meek."[17]

Although these definitions are true, they can inaccurately leave you feeling like you need to think less of yourself, that you need to think you are insignificant and inferior. God's Word assures us that is not the case. Each one of us is significant. We were all created by God with a very important purpose.

One of the Greek words used in the New Testament for humility is *praÿtēs* (prä-o'-tās), which means "meekness."[18] To paraphrase the definition of meekness as defined in the *Vines Complete Expository Dictionary:*[19] Meekness does not refer to only a person's outward behavior or their relations with other people or even to their natural disposition. It has a much fuller, deeper significance when used in Scripture than it does in Greek writings outside of Scripture. It is "an inwrought grace of the soul" that is displayed in one's actions towards God. "It is that temper of spirit in which we accept His dealings with us as good, and therefore without disputing or resisting." Meekness describes a condition of the mind and heart and it is the opposite of self-assertiveness and self-interest; "it is equanimity of spirit that is neither elated nor cast down, simply because it is not occupied with self at all."

Another Greek word that is used in the Bible for humility is *tapeinophrosynē* (tä-pā-no-fro-sü'-nā). My interpretation of the definition of this word is a deep understanding in the mind and the heart that we were created to serve others, to help lift them up and to have sympathy for them.

Three great authors described humility in this manner:

- "[A humble man] will not be thinking about humility: he will not be thinking about himself at all." –C.S. Lewis, *Mere Christianity*[20]

- "Humility is not thinking less of yourself; it is thinking of yourself less." –Rick Warren, *The Purpose Driven Life*[21]

- "Humility—true humility—isn't putting yourself down. It's recognizing that you owe everything to God. It's stepping into your destiny based not on who you are or what you can do but on who God is and what he will do through you." –Steven Furtick, *(UN)QUALIFIED*[22]

Is there a particular definition that stands out to you the most; that maybe gives you a new perspective on humility?

Journal any additional messages, thoughts, or ideas that God has placed on your heart:

Prayer Circles

Use your prayer circles today to seek an open mind and heart for what the Holy Spirit wants to reveal to you during this section. You may want to use Psalm 139:23–24 for one of your Bible verses.

Details:

Details:

Bible Verse:

Bible Verse:

Humility—Day 2

Pride is the opposite of humility. Pride is thinking of yourself, while humility is thinking of others. Pride is not just thinking too highly of yourself (arrogance), it is also when you are thinking too little of yourself (self-deprecation). In both cases, you are making "self" the center of your focus. When God is not the center of your focus then you are at risk of becoming prideful. God desires a humble spirit.

> He has shown you, O mortal, what is good. And what does the LORD require of you? To act justly and to love mercy and to walk humbly with your God. (Micah 6:8)

Why is being humble so important to God?

I think C.S. Lewis aptly answers this question in his book *Mere Christianity*:

"We must not think Pride is something that God forbids because He is offended at it, or that Humility is something He demands as due to His own dignity—as if God Himself was proud. He is not in the least worried about His dignity. The point is, He wants you to know Him: wants to give you Himself."[23]

God wants you to know Him! Pride is rebellion against God; it attributes the honor and glory to oneself instead of to God alone. It creates a barrier that keeps you from having an intimate relationship with God and truly knowing Him.

Romans 8:7 tells us, "The mind governed by the flesh is hostile to God; it does not submit to God's law, nor can it do so."

What are some current barriers of pride in your life; areas where the focus is on you rather than on God or on others? If you can't think of any, ask God to reveal any areas that may be hidden.

Journal any additional messages, thoughts, or ideas that God has placed on your heart:

Prayer Circles

Use your prayer circles for the barriers that you identified. Surrender them in prayer and ask God to help you replace these areas of pride with humility.

Details: Details:

Bible Verse: Bible Verse:

Transformational Tip #1: Focus on Jesus

Acknowledging issues doesn't mean that they go away. The many seeds of pride (jealousy, people-pleasing, arrogance, etc.) won't go away by admitting them or by focusing on them. Only Jesus can break those chains; only His grace is sufficient. Don't focus on your checklist and the things that you need to fix, or on what others are doing; focus on Jesus and what He wants you to do.

> But he said to me, "My grace is sufficient for you, for my power is made perfect in weakness." (2 Corinthians 12:9)

"As long as your own personality is what you are bothering about you are not going to Him at all. The very first step is to try to forget about the self altogether. Your real, new self (which is Christ's and also yours, and yours just because it is His) will not come as long as you are looking for it. It will come when you are looking for Him." –C.S. Lewis, *Mere Christianity*[24]

Keep Jesus as your focal point. Make Him the point of reference through which you view all things. When He is the center of your focus, then you can't be. The Bible tells us we can't serve two masters. Dark and light cannot exist together. When you are focused on Jesus, the Light will shine through you and the darkness will be unable to exist.

Whisper His name, "Jesus," to get your focus back on Him when it strays.

Humility—Day 3

A humble spirit shows itself in three ways:[25]

i.   Recognition of our sinfulness in the presence of our holy God

> "Woe to me!" I cried. "I am ruined! For I am a man of unclean lips, and I live among a people of unclean lips, and my eyes have seen the King, the LORD Almighty." (Isaiah 6:5)

ii.   Obedience to God

> Remember how the LORD your God led you all the way in the wilderness these forty years, to humble and test you in order to know what was in your heart, whether or not you would keep his commands. (Deuteronomy 8:2)

iii.   Submission to God

> Because your heart was responsive and you humbled yourself before God when you heard what he spoke against this place and its people, and because you humbled yourself before me and tore your robes and wept in my presence, I have heard you, declares the LORD. (2 Chronicles 34:27)

The Bible provides numerous examples of how humility manifests itself in our actions and behaviors. These actions and behaviors show the outward expression of our inward commitment to recognize our sinfulness, be obedient to God and submit to Him in all our ways. They can be used as indicators to warn us when the condition of our heart requires a humility check.

We are going to look at these actions and behaviors in two different groups. In the first group, the verses below show us how humility goes hand in hand with **gentleness, patience, compassion, kindness, peacefulness and harmony**.

Therefore, as God's chosen people, holy and dearly loved, clothe yourselves with compassion, kindness, humility, gentleness and patience. (Colossians 3:12)

Be completely humble and gentle; be patient, bearing with one another in love. Make every effort to keep the unity of the Spirit through the bond of peace. (Ephesians 4:2–3)

Live in harmony with one another. Do not be proud, but be willing to associate with people of low position. Do not be conceited. (Romans 12:16)

Do you have any areas in your life where you have lost your gentleness, patience, compassion, kindness, peacefulness, or harmony?

Choose one of the areas you listed above and reflect on it from the perspective of a humble spirit: Are you recognizing your need for Jesus due to your own sinfulness? Are you being obedient to God? Are you submitting to God?

Journal any additional messages, thoughts, or ideas that God has placed on your heart:

Prayer Circles

Based on your revelations, reflections, thoughts, and ideas, what or whom can you circle in prayer?

Details: Details:

Bible Verse: Bible Verse:

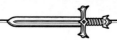

Transformational Tip #2: Stop Complaining, Pray Instead

Complaining puts all the focus on you; it takes you in a downward spiral into self-pity and rage. Complaints darken your perspective. Take your complaints to God; it shifts your focus and gives you a heavenly perspective. God is the only one who can handle your complaints without being tempted to slide into that pit with you. In the Bible, David showed us that it is okay to pour out our complaints to God:

> Hear me, my God, as I voice my complaint. (Psalm 64:1)

> I cry aloud to the LORD; I lift up my voice to the LORD for mercy. I pour out before him my complaint; before him I tell my trouble. (Psalm 142:1–2)

It will take intentionality to change this habit. You will need to practice self-awareness to catch any complaints that might slip out. Pray for the Holy Spirit to help you and to convict you when you mess up (please note that convict does not mean condemn; if you are feeling condemned that is <u>not</u> from the Holy Spirit). Also, ask people that you trust, that you would normally complain to, to help you by holding you accountable. Give them permission to stop you when you are complaining.

If your close circle of friends are complainers, you may need to rethink who you are allowing in your circle of influence. It is possible, that your friends may follow your lead and also stop complaining. If not, you may want to redefine your relationship with them. Pray for God to bring the right friends into your life.

> Do not be misled: "Bad company corrupts good character." (1 Corinthians 15:33)

> As iron sharpens iron, so one person sharpens another. (Proverbs 27:17)

Humility—Day 4

When we are having feelings that are making us lose our peacefulness, gentleness, kindness, compassion, patience, or harmony then it is time to do a heart check.

I find I lose basically all of these traits when I get offended or experience feelings of jealousy. Jealousy and offence come from the seed of pride. I will catch myself getting offended when somebody doesn't acknowledge me, or says something in a manner I deem offensive, or I am not included in something. What I have consistently found each time this occurs is that it is the state of my heart that is causing me to feel offended.

Offence occurs when your focus is on yourself rather than considering others and assuming the best about them. When you get offended and feel rejected, you are giving the enemy a seat at your table—the table that Jesus prepared specifically for you and for Him (Psalm 23:5).

Jealousy is a twisted version of focusing on yourself. Your focus is on others, but only to compare them to yourself and to covet their blessings. Comparison is a no-win activity; it will leave you feeling either superior or inferior. Both are prideful and will steal your peace, gentleness, kindness, compassion, patience, and harmony.

The tenth commandment tells us that we should not covet. When we covet, we are not trusting God with the gifts, abilities, and blessings that He has given us or the plans and the purpose that He has for us. We are saying that what He has given us isn't good enough. We are treating Him like a Father that has favorites and is holding out on us, rather than a good, good Father who does not change like shifting shadows and provides us with nothing but good and perfect gifts (James 1:17).

Is there an area of offence or jealousy that you are currently struggling with, or one you have had in the past?

Based on what has been discussed so far, can you now see that situation from a different perspective? If so, how has your perspective changed?

How will your actions change based on the new perspective (or how could they have changed)?

Journal any additional messages, thoughts, or ideas that God has placed on your heart:

Prayer Circles

Based on your revelations, reflections, thoughts, and ideas, what or whom can you circle in prayer?

Details:

Details:

Bible Verse:

Bible Verse:

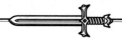

Transformational Tip #3: Be First to Apologize and ask for Forgiveness

Jesus tells us in Matthew 18:22, that we need to forgive seven times seventy times, and 1 Corinthians 13:5 says that love keeps no record of wrongs.

You can't control what other people do, but you can control your own actions. Apologizing is in your control. When you apologize, don't try to justify your actions, and be prepared that the other person may not be ready to accept your apology. Ask the Holy Spirit to guide you in this conversation.

Humility restores peace; maybe not always within the relationship as that requires acquiescence from the other party, but it will restore peace within your own heart.

I have heard it said that unforgiveness is like drinking poison and expecting the other person to die.

Unforgiveness plants seeds of bitterness in your heart. Forgiving doesn't mean you are agreeing with what they have said or done. If that person has hurt you, it doesn't mean you are saying what they did is okay. Forgiving them releases you from the bondage of unforgiveness. You are releasing it to God and freeing yourself from the weight of all the baggage that it brings.

Jesus showed us how important forgiveness is in Matthew 6:12, when He taught us how to pray: "And forgive us our debts, as we also have forgiven our debtors."

He went on to say that we will be forgiven by the Father *only* when we forgive others. I don't think the importance can be stressed any more than that.

> For if you forgive other people when they sin against you, your heavenly Father will also forgive you. But if you do not forgive others their sins, your Father will not forgive your sins. (Matthew 6:14–15)

Humility—Day 5

One of the fears I have struggled with is the fear of weakness. Or even worse—the fear of being perceived as weak. I have been in a continuous improvement cycle for years. And there are many positives that go with that. It is a good thing to have a teachable spirit and always be open to improvement. But, it is one thing to have a teachable spirit and another to have a fear of being weak (which is really a fear of not being in control), or a fear of being perceived as weak (which is a people-pleasing issue); both of which are rooted in pride. Since I equated being wrong with being weak, I felt it was important to strive to always be right.

I was reading the book *Like Yourself, Love Your Life* by Audrey Meisner, when I read a paragraph that was very convicting. It was explaining different expressions of people who are self-absorbed (The Player, Ms. Know-It-All, Mr. Important, and Miss Popular). Ms. Know-It-All is the one that jumped off the page at me: "This woman knows it ALL. She has the ability to fix everyone and gives herself free reign to correct anyone who doesn't line up with her system of values...In fact, she prides herself in helping everyone around her. By the way, she's always right, completely perfect, and has all the answers."[26]

I don't think I ever thought that I was perfect (although I was certainly striving for it), but I do believe that other people thought I did. I was very opinionated, and, yes, often did think that I was *helping*; however, let's be honest, sometimes it was just a matter of wanting to be right. This has caused me some huge problems in my relationships in the past. As Jesus continues to transform my heart and infuse me with humility, I am able to realize that I do not always have to be right. Humility means we lay down that need to be right, even if we are right. Our confidence comes from our Father and His Son who laid down His life for us to be redeemed, free and victorious—not from proving to other people that we are right.

One of the lessons I have learned is that we don't always need to share everything we know. Sometimes, prayer is all that is required. It can be very hard to watch others make poor choices when you know what the consequences will be on the other side of those decisions, but we need to let them have their own walk with God. Joyce Meyer says we can't control people; when we try to make them do what we want them to do, we are not leaving an opening for God to do what He needs to do. In addition, we should make sure we have the permission to speak into a person's life before offering any advice. Unsolicited feedback is often not welcomed.

Are there any areas in your life where you have a fear of not being in control? Or perhaps where you are striving to please people?

Do you have any unresolved conflicts because somebody won't agree that you are right? If so, lay down your need to be right. Apologize and ask for forgiveness.

Journal any additional messages, thoughts, or ideas that God has placed on your heart:

Prayer Circles

Based on your revelations, reflections, thoughts, and ideas, what or whom can you circle in prayer?

Details: Details:

Bible Verse: Bible Verse:

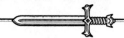

Transformational Tip #4: Give People the Benefit of the Doubt

Think the best of others and assume that they have the best intentions in mind.

A great quote from the movie, *Facing the Giants,* tells us that we can't judge others by their actions and ourselves by our intentions.[27] So often we make assumptions and jump to inaccurate conclusions. Offence or frustration with people occurs when we judge their actions or behaviors from a "self" focused perspective.

There are numerous stories that have circulated through social media or email that showcase this point. One example is a man riding a bus with his children. The children are being very rambunctious and annoying the other passengers. The man does nothing to control them, he just sits there quietly, oblivious to the disruption they are causing. As the story progresses, it is revealed that this family was coming from the hospital where their mother/wife had just passed away. Any feelings of annoyance immediately turned to sympathy and compassion.

This story reminds us that we don't know what other people are going through, what might be weighing on their minds and hearts.

Develop a habit of assuming that people have the best intentions in mind. Most often, their actions and behaviors are not about you at all.

> "Do not judge, or you too will be judged. For in the same way you judge others, you will be judged, and with the measure you use, it will be measured to you. Why do you look at the speck of sawdust in your brother's eye and pay no attention to the plank in your own eye?" (Matthew 7:1–3)

Humility—Day 6

The second group of actions and behaviors through which humility is expressed consists of **modesty, eagerness to serve, honesty, generosity, being an example to others**, and **submission**. These traits are evident in the verses below:

> Be shepherds of God's flock that is under your care, watching over them—not because you must, but because you are willing, as God wants you to be; not pursuing dishonest gain, but eager to serve; not lording it over those entrusted to you, but being examples to the flock. And when the Chief Shepherd appears, you will receive the crown of glory that will never fade away. In the same way, you who are younger, submit yourselves to your elders. All of you, clothe yourselves with humility toward one another, because, "God opposes the proud but shows favor to the humble." Humble yourselves, therefore, under God's mighty hand, that he may lift you up in due time. (1 Peter 5:2–6)

> Remind the people to be subject to rulers and authorities, to be obedient, to be ready to do whatever is good, to slander no one, to be peaceable and considerate, and to show true humility toward all men. (Titus 3:1–2)

Jesus walked on earth for thirty years before He was announced, showing us that you can be anointed without being announced. Our eagerness to serve should not depend on the visibility of the service. When we are feeling burned out and unappreciated because we are not getting recognized for the contribution we are making, that is a warning sign that pride is rearing its ugly head. God sees your contribution. Colossians 3:23 says, "Whatever you do, work at it with all your heart, as working for the Lord, not for human masters." We all appreciate recognition for a job well done, that is natural and healthy when it comes from a place of being delighted with having made a contribution that was praiseworthy. However, if you rely on that recognition from people in order to validate *you* as praiseworthy and determine *your* value, then you start to serve for the wrong reasons. A humble heart is willing to serve in an unseen, unpaid position and will readily submit (respectfully yield) to the leaders and authorities that God has put in place.

Do you have any areas in which you serve where you feel under-valued or under-appreciated?

If so, is it because you don't know if your contribution is praiseworthy or because you are basing your value on the praise?

Journal any revelations or perspective changes that God has placed on your heart:

Prayer Circles

Based on your revelations, reflections, thoughts, and ideas, what can you circle in prayer?

Details: Details:

Bible Verse: Bible Verse:

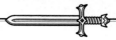

Transformational Tip #5: Serve

Having a servant's heart is synonymous to humility. The essence of a humble spirit is serving others. Therefore, it is only natural that serving is something we can do to develop a humble heart.

The act of serving lifts your focus from yourself and places it on others. It produces a double blessing, as most often you will be even more blessed than the person(s) you are serving.

Join a team at church. Be willing to serve wherever there is a need, not only based on your skill level or interests. If you are used to always leading, volunteer as part of a team in a non-leadership capacity. If there is need on a team that is not an area of interest for you, fill that need anyway. Be ready to fill in wherever needed.

Serving in God's house also gives you the benefits of developing deeper connections and being part of a team that is fulfilling a greater purpose, the plan that God has for His church.

> Whatever you do, work at it with all your heart, as working for the Lord, not for human masters, since you know that you will receive an inheritance from the Lord as a reward. It is the Lord Christ you are serving. (Colossians 3:23–24)

Humility—Day 7

Humility is an attitude of the heart that carries into all aspects of life. Pride is hidden in all the recesses of our heart and it is an ongoing process to replace it with humility in all the nooks and crannies.

When I decided to go to Bible college and leave behind my profession of twenty-eight years, it was a very humbling experience. Going from a management position within our local police service to stacking chairs and cleaning walls with a group of young adults that were anywhere from fifteen to thirty years younger than me was an opportunity for a lesson in humility!

One thing I learned during this shift in my life is that pride may be more easily recognizable in the operational or functional areas of our lives such as work, sports, hobbies, relationships, etc., than they are in our spiritual disciplines such as serving, praying, studying the Bible, and praising God. If we don't keep our hearts in check, we can become prideful even in our obedience to God.

"Our ego can never be defeated try as we might to bridle or bury it…Just when we think we are there and have won the battle, a truth pierces the darkness and we realize that the sin of pride has its roots even in excessive attempts to be humble." —Henry K. Ripplinger, *The Angelic Occurrence*[28]

Although that sounds discouraging, it goes on to say, "We must daily acknowledge our sinful and weak nature and become completely dependent upon Him. Only when we are aware of how far we fall short can we truly seek his strength and become an instrument of his peace."

This is a good reminder that pride is not something that we should strive to overcome. It will always be part of our nature. Instead, we need to recognize, acknowledge, and focus on our need for our Savior— every moment of every day. When we keep our focus on Jesus, we will start to become more like Him, with a gentle and humble heart. As we continually acknowledge our need for Jesus, we will start to submit to Him and obey Him, naturally, as a by-product of our need for Him.

"Take my yoke upon you and learn from me, for I am gentle and humble in heart, and you will find rest for your souls." (Matthew 11:29)

Do you have any areas of pride that may have seeped into your spiritual disciplines that you did not recognize previously because they were masked as obedience to God? If so, take this opportunity to thank Him for bringing this to your attention. Allow this realization to shift your focus to Jesus and your need for Him every moment of every day.

Journal any additional messages, thoughts, or ideas that God has placed on your heart:

Prayer Circles

Based on your revelations, reflections, thoughts, and ideas, what or whom can you circle in prayer?

Details:

Bible Verse:

Details:

Bible Verse:

Transformational Tip #6: Read the Bible with Jesus as the Central Character, not Yourself

Read the Bible with the perspective of what it will reveal about Jesus and His character, not from the perspective of what it can do for you.

The Bible has the answer to any problem that you have or issue that you are going through. Because of this, it is easy to fall into the trap of reading the Bible with the only intention of solving our own problems. Often we will associate ourselves with people in the Bible that really represent Jesus. I'm sure most people who have read the story of David and Goliath (1 Samuel 17) have put themselves as David slaying their giant. In actuality, we are the Israelites cowering in the background. It is Jesus that slays the giant! This story foreshadows the strength and courage that Jesus gives us to overcome our fears, obstacles and enemies.

Reading the Bible for practical application towards your life is great and necessary, but it should be secondary. The first question we should ask when reading the Bible is, "What does this tell me about Jesus?" Then ask the question, "How does this apply to me and my life?"

Humility—Day 8

As we develop a heart of humility, we get to know God more; and, as a result, our relationship deepens and we move further along the humility spectrum. The Bible shows us that there are several promises that come with a humble heart.

1. **Promotion**

   Jesus taught repeatedly that the humble would be raised up and those that try to promote themselves would be humbled. In three different teachings, Jesus used these same words: "For [all] those who exalt themselves will be humbled, and those who humble themselves will be exalted" (Matthew 23:12; Luke 14:11, 18:14). He also said, "Anyone who wants to be first must be the very last, and the servant of all" (Mark 9:35).

   The apostles continued this teaching as they were building the church.

   > Humble yourselves, therefore, under God's mighty hand, that he may lift you up in due time. (1 Peter 5:6)

   > Humble yourselves before the Lord, and he will lift you up. (James 4:10)

2. **Blessings**

   God promises these blessings will be received by the humble:

   i. *Favor/Grace*

      > But he gives us more grace. That is why Scripture says: "God opposes the proud but shows favor to the humble." (James 4:6)

      > He mocks proud mockers but shows favor to the humble and oppressed. (Proverbs 3:34)

   ii. *Wisdom*

      > When pride comes, then comes disgrace, but with humility comes wisdom. (Proverbs 11:2)

iii. *Honor*

> Wisdom's instruction is to fear the LORD, and humility comes before honor. (Proverbs 15:33)

> Before a downfall the heart is haughty, but humility comes before honor. (Proverbs 18:12)

iv. *Prosperity and Life*

> Humility is the fear of the LORD; its wages are riches and honor and life. (Proverbs 22:4)

Think of a time that you humbled yourself and reflect on how you were lifted up by that moment, and on any blessings that you received as a result. Journal your reflections and any additional messages, thoughts, or ideas that God has placed on your heart:

Prayer Circles

Based on your reflections, circle your blessings in a prayer of thanksgiving. Thank the Holy Spirit for the work He is doing to mold your heart into one that is gentle and humble.

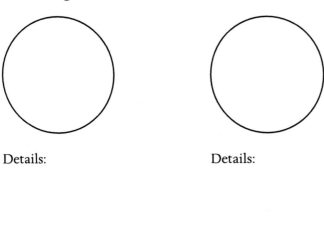

Details: Details:

Bible Verse: Bible Verse:

Humility—Day 9

When we have a humble heart, we get lifted up and receive the blessings of favor, wisdom, honor and prosperity. But God doesn't stop there, He also promises us the following:

3. **Protection**

> Seek the LORD, all you humble of the land, you who do what he commands. Seek righteousness, seek humility; perhaps you will be sheltered on the day of the LORD's anger. (Zephaniah 2:3)

> Then Hezekiah repented of the pride of his heart, as did the people of Jerusalem; therefore the LORD's wrath did not come on them during the days of Hezekiah. (2 Chronicles 32:26)

4. **Answered prayers**

> In his distress he sought the favor of the LORD his God and humbled himself greatly before the God of his ancestors. And when he prayed to him, the LORD was moved by his entreaty and listened to his plea. (2 Chronicles 33:12–13)

> Because your heart was responsive and you humbled yourself before the LORD when you heard what I have spoken against this place and its people—that they would become a curse and be laid waste—and because you tore your robes and wept in my presence, I also have heard you, declares the LORD. (2 Kings 22:19)

5. **Forgiveness and healing**

> If my people, who are called by my name, will humble themselves and pray and seek my face and turn from their wicked ways, then I will hear from heaven, and I will forgive their sin and will heal their land. (2 Chronicles 7:14)

6. **Deliverance**

> When the LORD saw that they humbled themselves, this word of the LORD came to Shemaiah: "Since they have

humbled themselves, I will not destroy them but will soon give them deliverance. My wrath will not be poured out on Jerusalem through Shishak." (2 Chronicles 12:7)

Because Rehoboam humbled himself, the LORD's anger turned from him, and he was not totally destroyed. (2 Chronicles 12:12)

God loves you! He wants to exalt you, bless you, shelter and protect you, answer your prayers, provide healing that comes with forgiveness, and save you from destruction, affliction, and distress.

Which of these promises resonates the most within your heart during this season of your life? Why?

Journal any additional messages, thoughts, or ideas that God has placed on your heart:

Prayer Circles

Based on your revelations, reflections, thoughts, and ideas, what can you circle in prayer?

Details: Details:

Bible Verse: Bible Verse:

Humility—Day 10 (Conclusion)

God wants you to know Him. These powerful words by C.S. Lewis, in *Mere Christianity,* illustrate the vital role that humility plays in this quest to know God: "But pride always means enmity—it *is* enmity. And not only enmity between man and man, but enmity to God...As long as you are proud you cannot know God."[29]

In *The Message,* Romans 8:6–8 says that focusing on self is the opposite of focusing on God. When we are not occupied with self, it enables God to lift us up; to bless us with favor, wisdom, honor and prosperity; to protect us, forgive us, and heal us; to save us from our troubles, and answer our prayers.

It is a humble heart that allows you to love God with all your heart, soul, strength, and mind, and to love your neighbor as yourself. Jesus told us that these are the two greatest commandments. If these commandments are kept, then all the other commandments and promises of the Bible will be fulfilled (Matthew 22:37–40).

As you remove prideful barriers and allow God's love for you into your heart, you will move closer and closer to the identity pivot point that transitions worldly humility to biblical humility—causing true and pure humility to flow from a transformed heart that is united with Christ.

> Therefore if you have any encouragement from being united with Christ, if any comfort from his love, if any common sharing in the Spirit, if any tenderness and compassion, then make my joy complete by being like-minded, having the same love, being one in spirit and of one mind. Do nothing out of selfish ambition or vain conceit. Rather, in humility value others above yourselves, not looking to your own interests but each of you to the interests of the others. In your relationships with one another, have the same mindset as Christ Jesus:
>
> > Who, being in very nature God,
> >   did not consider equality with God
> >   something to be used to his own advantage;

rather, he made himself nothing
    by taking the very nature of a servant,
    being made in human likeness.
And being found in appearance as a man,
    he humbled himself
    by becoming obedient to death—
    even death on a cross!
Therefore God exalted him to the highest place
    and gave him the name that is above every name,
that at the name of Jesus every knee should bow,
    in heaven and on earth and under the earth,
and every tongue acknowledge that Jesus Christ is Lord,
    to the glory of God the Father. (Philippians 2:1–11)

Journal any concluding messages, thoughts, or ideas that God has placed on your heart in regards to pride and humility:

Prayer Circles

Based on your revelations, reflections, thoughts, and ideas, what or whom can you circle in prayer?

Details: Details:

Bible Verse: Bible Verse:

CHURCH

God's House

As I write this I am about a week away from celebrating six years of salvation. In some ways, I find it hard to believe it was that long ago and in other ways it seems like maybe I did the math wrong and it was really sixteen years ago! To look back on what God has done in my life over the past six years leaves me overwhelmed and in awe. If you were to ask me what my feelings about church were six years ago, the answer would be quite different than it is now. And if you were to ask me twenty years ago, there would be an even larger difference! To give you a little bit of background, I will tell you the story of how I started going to church.

In 2004 and 2005, I played softball with some friends. I lived in the northeast part of Edmonton, Alberta and they lived in a small city just south of Edmonton called Leduc. I was at a point in my life where I wanted to move from where I was living and they convinced me to meet with their builder and consider building a house in Leduc. I ended up purchasing a lot that was on the same cul-de-sac as my friends. They were just ready to move in to their new home. About ten months later, we moved into our new home. When my daughter went and knocked on their door to play with their kids she was in for a surprise. She came back home and told me that they did not live there any more, they had moved! I couldn't believe it—it had been less than a year. They had not told me anything about moving. I didn't know what to think. Of course, looking back, I now know exactly what to think—you will see what I mean. My daughter, Danielle, became friends with the young girl of the new family that had moved in and after a few years this young girl started attending City Life Church. I bet you know where I am going with this now! After a while she started inviting Danielle to go to the youth group at church. One Saturday night after youth group, Danielle came home and asked me if she could go to church the next day. It just so happened that it was Easter weekend. I didn't feel I could very well say no to this request but I told her that I would go with her. Now I am sure that part of me was also seeking, but I didn't know that. My biggest reason for going was to check out this church that my teenage daughter wanted to attend—I wanted to make sure it wasn't some kind of a cult where they were going to make her "drink the kool-aid" (for those that aren't familiar with this saying, it refers to a cult in Jonestown back in 1978 where over nine-hundred people died after being ordered by the leader, Jim Jones, to drink kool-aid laced with poison). So, on April 4, 2010 I walked into City Life Church in Leduc, with my daughter, and I have never been the same since!

Although we continued to attend church each week, it was eight months before I accepted Jesus as my Lord and Savior. It was even longer before I started to trust the church. And it wasn't until I went to Bible college that I truly realized the importance of the church to Jesus; how loving Jesus and loving the church could not be separated.

I grew up in a family that had a deep distrust and dislike of churches. We never talked about Jesus when I was growing up, so I had no idea what my parents thought about Him, but I did "know" that churches were bad. It wasn't until recently that I better understood the reasons behind their combined feelings of indifference and animosity. I am not going to get into those reasons as that is not my story to tell; however, suffice it to say that their experiences with who they thought was Jesus (through His supposed followers) and church were drastically different than mine have been. This fueled a fire that was already slowly burning inside of me. A passion to help Christians find their true identity in Christ so that people will be drawn to the real Jesus that shines through them. As Christ-followers, we *are* the church and we represent Jesus to those who don't know Him. It pains me to think that I could be the reason that somebody hardens their heart toward Jesus and His church. I want everybody to know the real Jesus: the loving, gracious, merciful, faithful, compassionate, generous Jesus that I know! And to see His church as an extension of the incredible Jesus that He is.

> My goal is that they may be encouraged in heart and united in love,
> so that they may have the full riches of complete understanding,
> in order that they may know the mystery of God, namely, Christ,
> in whom are hidden all the treasures of wisdom and knowledge.
> (Colossians 2:2–3)

I like this quote from C.S. Lewis in *Mere Christianity*: "When we Christians behave badly, or fail to behave well, we are making Christianity unbelievable to the outside world."[30]

To make Christianity believable to the outside world, we need to spread the aroma of Him everywhere we go (2 Corinthians 2:14). We can only spread the true aroma of Jesus when we are walking in His image, in our identity in Christ. Church plays a vital role in finding that true identity. It is only through a healthy community of believers in a Jesus-centered, Bible-based church that you can fulfill the plan and the purpose that God has created you for. Together we become what we could not be alone.

> How lovely is your dwelling place, LORD Almighty! My soul yearns, even faints, for the courts of the LORD; my heart and my flesh cry out for the living God. Even the sparrow has found a home, and the swallow a nest for herself, where she may have her young—a place near your altar, LORD Almighty, my King and my God. Blessed are those who dwell in your house; they are ever praising you. (Psalm 84:1–4)

Church—Day 1

When God created Adam and Eve they were able to meet with God and delight in the glory of His presence. They got to walk with Him in the Garden of Eden. Imagine how great that would have been! But, because of their disobedience, sin entered the world and separated all of mankind from God. God wants us to be near Him. He created us because He loves us. He wants to be able to meet with us.

In the Old Testament times, the times before Jesus was born, first the tabernacle and then the temple were built so God could dwell among His people. These were the places used to bridge the separation between man and God. This is where people would bring their sacrifices in order to seek forgiveness and to worship God. But only the priests that were chosen by God could offer the sacrifice to Him and enter His sacred dwelling. During this time, the priests would carry the message of the people to God and the prophets would carry the message of God to the people. Jesus changed all that. He died, as the final sacrifice, for our sins and rose again to leave us with the Holy Spirit who lives in us. Jesus reconciled each one of us to God—He is the only bridge that closes the gap between us. Through Jesus, we are now able to worship God freely anytime, anywhere. We don't need specific anointed priests to intercede on our behalf (however, God uses our pastors and church leaders to teach and guide us on our journey), or prophets to relay the message from God to us (although God still uses prophets and other people as one of the many ways that He speaks to us, but it is the Holy Spirit within us that discerns the messages from God). Jesus is our intercessor. Through Him we are all anointed. And through Him we can all hear God's gentle whispers (1 Kings 19:12).

> "Then have them make a sanctuary for me, and I will dwell among them." (Exodus 25:8)

> All this is from God, who reconciled us to himself through Christ and gave us the ministry of reconciliation: that God was reconciling the world to himself in Christ, not counting people's sins against them. And he has committed to us the message of reconciliation. God made him who had no sin to be sin for us,

so that in him we might become the righteousness of God. (2 Corinthians 5:18–19, 21)

You can have a personal relationship with the Creator of the universe because, through Jesus, you are now the righteousness of God! God wants you to be near Him. Do you feel near to God?

What does it mean to you that Jesus reconciled you to God and gave you the ministry of reconciliation?

Journal any additional messages, thoughts, or ideas that God has placed on your heart:

Prayer Circles

Based on your revelations, reflections, thoughts, and ideas, what or whom can you circle in prayer?

Details: Details:

Bible Verse: Bible Verse:

Church—Day 2

So, if I am reconciled with God and can worship Him from the comfort of my own home and have a relationship with Him on my own, then why is church vital to finding my true identity in Christ?

To answer this, let's begin by looking at the meaning of the word *church* and the creation of the New Testament church in Acts 2.

The Greek word that is used for church in the New Testament is *ekklēsia* (ek-klā-sē'-ä); this means the called out, or the gathered together.[31] The *Holman Illustrated Bible Dictionary* states that it "refers to any assembly, local bodies of believers, or the universal body of all believers." It goes on to describe the church as the people of God in this way: "Redemptive history demonstrates that God's purposes are not limited to redemption of individuals. Instead, God's intent was to form a people (Gen. 12:1–3)."[32]

Just before Jesus ascended back to heaven, He told the apostles to stay in Jerusalem and wait until they were baptized with the Holy Spirit (Acts 1:4–5). Immediately after being baptized with the Holy Spirit, Peter stood up and preached a powerful message with his new anointing, and 3,000 people became followers of Jesus Christ. And, as a group of believers, they started to gather together. This was the initiation of the church.

> The community continually committed themselves to learning what the apostles taught them, gathering for fellowship, breaking bread, and praying. Everyone felt a sense of awe because the apostles were doing many signs and wonders among them. There was an intense sense of togetherness among all who believed; they shared all their material possessions in trust. They sold any possessions and goods *that did not benefit the community* and used the money to help everyone in need. They were unified as they worshiped at the temple day after day. In homes, they broke bread and shared meals with glad and generous hearts. The new disciples praised God, and they enjoyed the goodwill of all the people *of the city*. Day after day the Lord added to their number everyone who was experiencing liberation. (Acts 2:42–27 The Voice)

There was an **intense sense of togetherness** among all who believed and they were experiencing liberation!

How do your thoughts of church resemble the description in Acts 2:42–47? How does it differ?

Journal any additional messages, thoughts, or ideas that God has placed on your heart:

Prayer Circles

Based on your revelations, reflections, thoughts, and ideas, what or whom can you circle in prayer?

Details:

Details:

Bible Verse:

Bible Verse:

Transformational Tip #1: Find a Jesus-Centered, Bible-Based Church

If you do not already have a local church to call home, find one. When shopping for a church, make sure you know what the church believes. Here are the key beliefs to look for in a healthy, evangelical church:

- There is only one true God, the Creator of heaven and earth
- Jesus is the only way to God
- The Trinity: God the Father, Jesus Christ the Son and Holy Spirit
- Jesus was 100% man and 100% God
- Jesus died to pay the penalty for our sins and rose again on the third day to give those who believe eternal life
- Scripture is the divinely inspired Word of God and the **absolute** authority of truth

"You are my witnesses," declares the LORD, "and my servant whom I have chosen, so that you may know and believe me and understand that I am he. Before me no god was formed, nor will there be one after me." (Isaiah 43:10)

Jesus answered, "I am the way and the truth and the life. No one comes to the Father except through me." (John 14:6)

"All this I have spoken while still with you. But the Advocate, the Holy Spirit, whom the Father will send in my name, will teach you all things and will remind you of everything I have said to you." (John 14:25–26)

For God so loved the world that he gave his one and only Son, that whoever believes in him shall not perish but have eternal life. For God did not send his Son into the world to condemn the world, but to save the world through him. (John 3:16–17)

Your word, LORD, is eternal; it stands firm in the heavens. (Psalm 119:89)

Sanctify them by the truth; your word is truth. (John 17:17)

Church—Day 3

We have seen that there was an intense sense of togetherness when the church first began. They committed to continually learn, gather for fellowship, break bread, and pray *together*. They were unified.

God's plan for us is not as separate individuals that are unified through the blood of Christ, but as a part of the body of Christ, which is the church. The plan and purpose He has for us as individuals will be directly related to His plan for the church. The intent of Jesus is to make known the manifold wisdom of God—*through* the church (Ephesians 3:10).

> For just as each of us has one body with many members, and these members do not all have the same function, so in Christ we, though many, form one body, and each member belongs to all the others. (Romans 12:4–5)

We are all part of one body, with Christ as the head. Each of us plays a significant role to make that body function as it was designed. The church needs *you*, otherwise the body is missing a body part. It doesn't matter what body part you are; what matters is that you are connected to the body.

It is important to note that the body of Christ is not only referring to the universal church but also applies to each local church. In 1 Corinthians 12, Paul wrote to the local church in Corinth to teach them that God had given each member specific gifts to build each other up for the glory of Christ through His body, the church.

Read 1 Corinthians 12.

What gifts and abilities has God given you that can help build up the church?

Is church something you try to squeeze in around your other activities or is it a priority in your life?

Journal any additional messages, thoughts, or ideas that God has placed on your heart:

Prayer Circles

Based on the answers to your reflection questions, what can you circle in prayer today? Maybe how your gifts can be used, or your priorities adjusted?

Details: Details:

Bible Verse: Bible Verse:

We have seen the importance of each part to the body of Christ, His church. It is also critical that we understand the importance that the body has on each part.

> So Christ himself gave the apostles, the prophets, the evangelists, the pastors and teachers, to equip his people for works of service, so that the body of Christ may be built up until we all reach unity in the faith and in the knowledge of the Son of God and become mature, attaining to the whole measure of the fullness of Christ. Then we will no longer be infants, tossed back and forth by the waves, and blown here and there by every wind of teaching and by the cunning and craftiness of people in their deceitful scheming. Instead, speaking the truth in love, we will grow to become in every respect the mature body of him who is the head, that is, Christ. From him the whole body, joined and held together by every supporting ligament, grows and builds itself up in love, as each part does its work. (Ephesians 4:11–16)

As the scriptures above tell us, the body of Christ, the church, is imperative in order to mature and reach unity in the faith and in the knowledge of Jesus. The church grows our wisdom and ability to discern false teaching and deceitful schemes. It is only by being connected to the body that we will be able to grow and mature in His teachings to attain the full extent of His likeness—to be transformed into the fullness of the image of Christ. Our faith will not mature—and therefore, will not last—if we try to do it alone. We need our spiritual family to help us reach the destiny that God has created us for. We, as a *part* of the body, cannot function as designed if we are not *connected* to the body.

In Matthew 28:18–20, Jesus did not say to go and make disciples of all people. He said to go and make disciples of all *nations*. This is a command to His church. The *Holman Illustrated Bible Dictionary* describes it like this: "Thus, obedience to the Great Commission (Matt. 28:16–20) is not simply a function of the church but is essential to her identity as the people of God."[33] And the notes in the *Life Application Study Bible* for Ephesians 4:12–13 offer this additional insight: "God has given his church

127

an enormous responsibility—to make disciples in every nation (Matthew 28:18–20)…If we had to fulfill this command as individuals, we might as well give up without trying—it would be impossible. But God calls us as members of his body…Together we can obey God more fully than any of us could alone. It is a human tendency to overestimate what we can do by ourselves and to underestimate what we can do as a group. But as the body of Christ, we can accomplish more together than we would dream possible working by ourselves. Working together, the church can express the fullness of Christ."[34]

Can you think of a time when you overestimated what you thought you could do on your own? Or maybe a time when you accomplished more as a group than you thought possible?

Have you been trying to walk your faith journey on your own? Maybe slipping in and out of church each week but never really connecting?

Journal any additional messages, thoughts, or ideas that God has placed on your heart:

Prayer Circles

Based on your revelations, reflections, thoughts, and ideas, what or whom can you circle in prayer?

Details: Details:

Bible Verse: Bible Verse:

Transformational Tip #2: Make a One-Time Commitment to be Planted in Your Church

> The righteous will flourish like a palm tree, they will grow like a cedar of Lebanon; planted in the house of the LORD, they will flourish in the courts of our God. (Psalm 92:12–13)

When you plant a tree in fertile soil it flourishes. If you dig up that tree and replant it somewhere else, its growth is stunted for a while; it will likely come back and grow again but possibly never to the extent that it would have grown had it stayed planted. Also, if it continues to be uprooted and moved it will eventually wither and die; it is the same with our faith. Once you have found a healthy Jesus-centered, Bible-based church, don't let offence uproot you.

Know going in that you will at some point be offended—church is made up of people and people are not perfect. Often we project offence that was never even there; it is our own pride, insecurities, or just plain old stuff that we are dealing with that causes us to feel offended. The enemy will jump on those feelings and attack you in that area; he will hit you when you are down. Satan knows the power of church and will do whatever he can to keep you from growing deep roots. Don't let him win! Jesus already defeated him on the cross (Colossians 2:15) and has given you victory! All you have to do is receive it.

Maybe you haven't been offended by anybody, but you find you like the worship in one church, the message in another, and the kids programs in another. This is like being a tree planted in a pot so it can move around easily. Its roots are restricted; therefore, the growth of that tree will be restricted. Instead of going from church to church trying to feed your own wants and desires, commit to one church that you call home and help build it to be all that God has called it to be. Maybe you are that missing body part that is keeping the church from developing in a particular area.

It is important to note that sometimes people are called by God to move; that is completely different than leaving because of offence or not committing because of our own selfish desires. If you are called to move,

God will make it clear; not only to you but to the leaders, mentors, and friends in your church also, and you will be encouraged and supported to follow the path God has for you.

> But I am like an olive tree flourishing in the house of God; I trust in God's unfailing love for ever and ever. (Psalm 52:8)

Church—Day 5

God made us as a community. He designed us to do life together; to love one another and to love His church, just as He loves it. In addition to being the body of Christ, the church is referred to in Scripture as the bride of Christ. We can't love Jesus without loving His bride.

> Husbands, love your wives, just as Christ loved the church and gave himself up for her to make her holy, cleansing her by the washing with water through the word, and to present her to himself as a radiant church, without stain or wrinkle or any other blemish, but holy and blameless. (Ephesians 5:25–27)

> "Let us rejoice and be glad and give him glory! For the wedding of the Lamb has come, and his bride has made herself ready. Fine linen, bright and clean, was given her to wear." (Fine linen stands for the righteous acts of God's holy people.) (Revelation 19:7–8)

As the church, we need to make ourselves ready. We need to clothe ourselves with the righteous acts of God's holy people. We can't do this if we are divided. There is nothing more divisive than being against that which Jesus died to build—His church.

> So that there should be no division in the body, but that its parts should have equal concern for each other. If one part suffers, every part suffers with it; if one part is honored, every part rejoices with it. Now you are the body of Christ, and each one of you is a part of it. (1 Corinthians 12:25–27)

It is important to see the church the way Jesus sees it. It will never be perfect; it can't be, as it is made up of imperfect people. But, just as God sees us as righteous through the lens of Jesus, we need to see the church through the grace that He has lavishly poured out on us. As you receive His free gift of grace, it will flow through you, both to individuals and to His church.

What is the current state of your heart towards church?

Have you had a bad experience with people that has caused you to have bad feelings towards the church? If so, have you forgiven those people?

Journal any additional messages, thoughts, or ideas that God has placed on your heart:

Prayer Circles

Use your prayer circles today to forgive anybody in church who may have offended you or hurt you. Ask God to help you see them and His church the way He sees them.

Details: Details:

Bible Verse: Bible Verse:

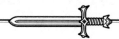

Transformational Tip #3: Take Ownership

When you are planted in a church, it is your home. It is your responsibility to make it great. We aren't just made for something great, we are part of something great by being part of the church.

When you notice gaps, fill them. Pick up that garbage on the floor, clean the bathroom if it is dirty, help set up chairs; don't think it is not your role because you are not on the team assigned to those duties. Have eyes that see the details that will make the experience for your guests be the best it can be and have the heart to take the action required. Most importantly, make your guests feel welcome. It is *your* responsibility to welcome them into your home; regardless of whether or not you are on the greeting team.

We don't go to church; we *are* the church. We need to protect God's House like we protect our own heart.

> For zeal for your house consumes me, and the insults of those who insult you fall on me. (Psalm 69:9)

In the Bible, in the Book of Ezra, chapters 3 to 6, the temple was being rebuilt after being destroyed by Nebuchadnezzar. Those that were rebuilding the temple had great opposition against them. But they stood strong in their faith and did not let the opposition sidetrack them from the work that God called them to do. When asked who authorized them to rebuild the temple, they responded in Ezra 5:11 with: "We are the servants of the God of heaven and earth, and we are rebuilding the temple."

We are all servants of the God of heaven and earth and we are called as part of the body of Christ to build the church. What an amazing honor and privilege He has bestowed upon us!

> Better is one day in your courts than a thousand elsewhere; I would rather be a doorkeeper in the house of my God than dwell in the tents of the wicked. (Psalm 84:10)

Church—Day 6

Being committed to a healthy Jesus-centered, Bible-based church inspires us to live well. It instills in us a sense of purpose and provides us with values that will make us healthy. It is the condition of our soul and spirit that determines the quality of our life. Church is the healthiest possible environment for our spirit to grow. Once our spirit grows to be the largest of our three-part being (body, soul and spirit), then our soul and body will be led by the Holy Spirit—the ultimate condition for which we were designed!

God tells us that He has a plan and a purpose for our life (Jeremiah 29:11); that He has created us to do good works, which He has prepared in advance for us to do (Ephesians 2:10). The church is needed to fulfill this purpose, as Jesus was appointed to be head over everything *for* the church. It is through the church that the fullness of Jesus is revealed.

> And God placed all things under his feet and appointed him to be head over everything for the church, which is his body, the fullness of him who fills everything in every way. (Ephesians 1:22–23)

Church is also an environment where we challenge and encourage one another. This allows us to learn and grow to be all that God has called us to be. It is an atmosphere that is safe in which to learn the hard lessons in life such as letting go of bitterness and unforgiveness. It is where we find acceptance and belonging.

> Blessed are those you choose and bring near to live in your courts! We are filled with the good things of your house, of your holy temple. (Psalm 65:4)

If you are established in a church, what blessings has this provided for you (i.e. areas of growth, opportunities, relationships, etc.)?

If you are not actively participating in a thriving church family, what is holding you back?

Journal any additional messages, thoughts, or ideas that God has placed on your heart:

Prayer Circles

Use your prayer circles today for prayers of thanksgiving for your church. If you don't have a church, pray for the Holy Spirit to guide you to one.

Details: Details:

Bible Verse: Bible Verse:

Church—Day 7

Church is not only meant to connect with God, it is also meant to connect with each other. The Bible refers to this as fellowship. Fellowship is an essential ingredient in our sanctification process; our identity in Christ is incomplete without it. In 1 John 1:3, it is clear that our fellowship with each other must be centered around our relationship with Jesus.

> We proclaim to you what we have seen and heard, so that you also may have fellowship with us. And our fellowship is with the Father and with his Son, Jesus Christ. (1 John 1:3)

I like the way the *The Voice Bible* paraphrases it. It shows that as followers of Jesus Christ, we become a united family.

> What we saw and heard we pass on to you so that you, too, will be connected with us intimately *and become family*. Our family is united by our connection with the Father and His Son Jesus, the Anointed One. (1 John 1:3 The Voice)

The Greek word that is used for fellowship in the New Testament is *koinōnia* (koi-nō-nē'-ä). The *One-Volume Illustrated Edition Zondervan Bible Commentary* describes fellowship as follows: "Fellowship (*koinōnia*) indicates an openhearted sharing in which each believer gave to others what he had himself received, whether of spiritual or material blessings."[35] The first instance of this word in the New Testament is in Acts 2:42; the same place, as we learned earlier, that the church first began. Church is woven into the very fabric of fellowship.

Church is about doing life with our brothers and sisters in Christ; supporting and encouraging each other through the hard times and celebrating together in the good times. It is also about holding each other accountable; letting our love motivate us to help one another be all that God has called us to be. I have both witnessed and received these outpourings of love from church family time and time again. The beauty of it is beyond words. As Jacob said in Genesis 28:17, "This is none other than the house of God; this is the gate of heaven."

What does your life look like Monday through Saturday (i.e. your schedule, friends, activities, conversations, etc.)?

Do you connect with people from church outside of Sunday? If not, why not?

Journal any additional messages, thoughts, or ideas that God has placed on your heart:

Prayer Circles

Based on your revelations, reflections, thoughts, and ideas, what or whom can you circle in prayer?

Details: Details:

Bible Verse: Bible Verse:

Transformational Tip #4: Join a Connect Group

When I first started attending church, I continued to go because my daughter was going. I was so far out of my comfort zone trying to talk to people in this new environment. In fact, often my mind would go completely blank when somebody spoke to me and I could not for the life of me put together two words let alone a complete sentence! Since I had become "born again" later in life, there was an awkward transition from my old life to my new. The things that I used to do and say no longer seemed fun or appropriate. And although I still loved my friends, I was no longer comfortable with the activities or conversations that would take place. I gradually stopped attending the functions and activities that used to be such a huge part of my life (not only because it was uncomfortable but mostly to make time for me to pursue Jesus through connect groups and other church activities). I had been attending church regularly for about a year and a half when I started to pray for friendships within the church—up to this point I had no friendships of my own, I was riding on my daughter's coattails.

It was not long after I started praying this prayer that I received an invitation to be part of a discipleship group with our Lead Pastor. That changed everything for me! And shortly after the discipleship group started, I also joined a ladies connect group (also known as small groups). It was my very first Bible study! It was a Beth Moore study on the Book of Daniel. Not a very light topic to begin your Bible study adventure! In fact, I started exactly half way through so they were just beginning the eschatology (which is the study of end times) portion of the study— not a recommended place for new believers to start! It was that Bible study that started my unquenchable thirst for God's Word! But it was the relationships that I made within the two groups that strengthened my faith and kept me coming to church. I believe that if I had not made those connections, I eventually would have stopped going to church. My thirst for God's Word would have gradually diminished and I am certain I would have been pulled back into the distractions of the world.

I have learned in church that we need both circles and rows. The circles being the connect groups, and the rows being the church services. In rows, we are inspired, united in strength, and entertained; in circles, we are empowered, strengthened, and transformed.

> But if we walk in the light, as he is in the light, we have fellowship with one another, and the blood of Jesus, his Son, purifies us from all sin. (1 John 1:7)

> The temple I am going to build will be great, because our God is greater than all other gods. (2 Chronicles 2:5)

Our God is beyond compare! The awe and wonder of the Creator of the universe is more than my finite brain can fathom! The house we are building has to be the best, because our God is the best! God has given all of us the amazing honor of building His house to reach those who do not yet know Him and to strengthen and mature those who do. In order to do this, we need to be able to remove any distractions that may keep people from saying "yes" to Jesus, whether it is their first "yes" or their next "yes". We are most often the biggest distraction. Although we want the building and the programs to be excellent (let's face it, people's impression of God will not be great if they walk into a dirty building that is not taken care of and programs that have had no thought or planning put into them), ultimately God's House is not a building and it is not the programs—it is the people.

I have heard Brian Houston, the Senior Pastor of Hillsong Church, say that "church is not built on the talent and gifts of a few but on the sacrifice of many." As we have seen, we all play an important part in building God's house. Each of us needs to bring our best. Giving our best means that our hearts must be engaged; the church functions when our heart is in it. God sent Jesus with no strings attached. As humans we attach all kinds of conditions. To give our best we need to give without expectation of what we will receive in return; we need to give with no strings attached. I heard one of my pastors say that our best is not on a platform, it is getting on hands and knees to become a platform for someone else. I find that statement so powerful! We are here to lift others up, to help them become all that God has called them to be.

Isaiah 54:2 tells us that in order to enlarge our tent we can't hold back; we need to lengthen our cord and strengthen our stakes. We can't coast on our best of yesterday. We need to continually stretch and grow in our gifts and abilities. Your best today should not look like your best tomorrow; as you learn and grow your best will change.

Where are you at right now? Are you giving your best to the house of God?

Are you being intentional to grow in your gifts and abilities?

Journal any additional messages, thoughts, or ideas that God has placed on your heart:

Prayer Circles

Based on your revelations, reflections, thoughts, and ideas, what or whom can you circle in prayer?

Details: Details:

Bible Verse: Bible Verse:

Transformational Tip #5: Commit to Personal Growth for Corporate Gain

Personal growth is fundamental for fulfillment. We will always have areas in which we need to grow. It is the stretching and growing that propels us forward into the spacious life that God has for us (Psalm 18:19).

Often we will commit to growth to reap the benefits in our personal lives. It may be to get a promotion or a different job, to make a certain sports team, to improve our relationships within our family or at work, or for our own satisfaction. These are all good things, but they are all temporary things.

Church is God's eternal plan. When we commit to our own personal growth for the benefit of the church, we are committing to building eternity with God. Therefore, it is not personal growth in itself that will provide fulfillment, but the purpose for which we use that growth that will give us the gratification that our heart desires. And as an offshoot of this fulfillment, we will also receive benefits in our personal lives.

> But seek first his kingdom and his righteousness, and all these things will be given to you as well. (Matthew 6:33)

> So it is with you. Since you are eager for gifts of the Spirit, try to excel in those that build up the church. (1 Corinthians 14:12)

Church—Day 9 (Conclusion)

When we confess with our mouth that Jesus is Lord and believe in our heart that God raised Him from the dead, we are saved (Romans 10:9): We become believers, part of the universal body of the church. This note from *The Voice Bible* in regards to Philippians 2:1–11 describes the church beautifully:[36]

> "Paul describes a community where every person considers the needs of others first and does nothing from selfishness; it pulls together rather than pulls apart, and it is a body that knows its purpose and lets nothing interfere with it. It is an extended spiritual family where others line up to become part of this sacred assembly and to make it their home because they feel encouragement and know they are truly loved. So Paul urges the Philippians to strive for this radical unity and fulfill his joy by having the mind of Jesus who humbled Himself, became a servant, and suffered the death of the cross. Jesus becomes the example of humility and service, leading to the kind of unity Paul imagines."

To achieve this radical unity, you must be connected to the body, which is the local church. Otherwise, you are a body part that is disconnected, and unable to perform the function for which you were created. Being planted in a local church is not a requirement for your salvation, as we saw above in Romans 10:9; but, it is a requirement to fulfill the plan and purpose that God has created you for.

In Matthew 16:16–18, Jesus declares that His church will be built on the faith that Peter demonstrated in Jesus as the Son of the living God and that not even the gates of Hades will be able to overcome it. Church is the pillar and foundation of the truth (1 Timothy 3:15); it is built on the foundation of the apostles and prophets, with Jesus as the cornerstone (Ephesians 2:20).

We are now playing our part in the history of the church. We are writing our chapter into His story. How will it read to our children, and our children's children? What legacy of the church will we leave behind?

One thing I ask from the LORD, this only do I seek: that I may dwell in the house of the LORD all the days of my life, to gaze on the beauty of the LORD and to seek him in his temple. (Psalm 27:4)

Journal any concluding messages, thoughts, or ideas that God has placed on your heart about church:

Prayer Circles

Based on your revelations, reflections, thoughts, and ideas, what or whom can you circle in prayer?

Details: Details:

Bible Verse: Bible Verse:

IDENTITY

Embracing Your True Identity

In the New Testament, the phrase "in Christ" occurs approximately eighty times (the number varies a little up or down depending on the translation used). Second Corinthians 5:17 states, "Therefore, if anyone is in Christ, the new creation has come: The old has gone, the new is here!" When I first accepted Jesus as my Lord and Savior, I was ecstatic that I was a new creation. I completely embraced all the new things that God was teaching me. I thought I understood what it meant for me to be in Christ; my salvation, accepting Jesus into my heart, meant I was in Christ.

But, just like reading the Bible, when we think we understand something, God reveals a deeper level of meaning. God loves us so much that He will only reveal what we can handle at the moment. He will not overwhelm us by exposing us to everything we have to learn all at once. I soon realized that there was much more to being "in Christ" than I originally thought. To peel back more layers to this mystery, there were many issues I still had to work through. Often, we will think we have dealt with an issue only to have it resurface, taking us to another level of understanding and deepening our relationship with Jesus. I once heard this process explained using the metaphor of a diamond. The way a diamond is cut causes it to refract light differently at every angle. Every area of our life that requires growth (which, let's face it, is every area because if it doesn't require growth then it is likely not worth having), needs to be viewed from all the different angles giving us new and glorious insight with each twist and turn.

The pain of some of these new revelations was more memorable than others. At some points, rather than looking at an already cut diamond, it felt like I was going through the cutting process. There are three main areas that God revealed to me in which I was wearing masks that hid my true identity in Christ. The first mask was revealed when I flew with my daughter to the other side of the world to drop her off at Bible college. For almost seventeen years I had raised her on my own. It had been just the two of us. Then, suddenly, I was going to be on my own with a vast ocean separating us. At times, it hurt so much that it felt like a physical part of my body had been removed. But during this time, God showed me how a large part of my identity had been in my daughter, not in Him. I had been on a destructive path before I became pregnant. God sent me my baby to save me from that destruction before I acknowledged the real baby that He sent as my Savior. After years of using my daughter as my savior, it was time to shift that focus to Jesus.

About a year and a half later, the second mask was exposed: my performance. Actually, it resurfaced; I had realized earlier in my walk with Jesus that I had a problem with performance. I recognized that I was striving in the corporate world, in sports, and in parenting. I thought I had dealt with that and no longer put my identity in how I performed; however, in reality, I had just transferred it into my faith walk—my devotions, my Bible study, my church life, my serving. I had not removed the mask; I had just made it look prettier.

Only a few months after this revelation, as I neared the end of Bible college, I started to feel empty. I felt purposeless. I could not think of a single gifting that I had or contribution that I could bring to building God's kingdom and carrying out His plan. I concluded that my purpose must be finished. Maybe raising my daughter was my purpose and now I was done. This is when God showed me that I was putting my identity in my title and status. My daughter was living across the world, I no longer had my job title and position of authority, and I soon would be done college so could not be considered a student anymore either. What was I supposed to call myself? Who was I if I didn't have some sort of title or label to apply?

At these times, I felt completely alone, rejected and unworthy. But one thing that I am confident in declaring is that nothing overcomes an identity crisis like the truth of God's Word. There is no retail therapy (sports car or otherwise), extreme sport, substance, makeover, job, or relationship that will ever resolve your identity crisis—only Jesus can! Only the One who created you can help you understand who you were created to be. Each of these masks needed to be removed in order to move closer to my true identity in Christ.

It is only through embracing your true identity in Christ that you are able to fulfill the plan and the purpose that God has for your life and be transformed into His likeness.

For we are God's handiwork, created in Christ Jesus to do good works, which God prepared in advance for us to do. (Ephesians 2:10)

And we, who with unveiled faces all reflect the Lord's glory, are being transformed into his likeness with ever-increasing glory, which comes from the Lord, who is the Spirit. (2 Corinthians 3:18)

Identity—Day 1

So, what does it really mean to have your identity in Christ? It means that you receive your identity from Jesus and what He did for you on the cross, not from anything else. That your value and your worth come from God alone. It means you are not defined by your job, your title, your status, your children, your spouse, your looks, your skills and abilities, your accomplishments, your intellect, or your money. The only title that defines you is "child of God."

Over the course of your lifetime, many people have had opinions about who you are. Parents, teachers, friends, spouses, coaches, managers, boyfriends, or girlfriends have all made their assessment of you. This has influenced your own assessment of who you are. Any point of view that does not line up with what God says is contrary to the truth—it is simply a lie. You are not what anybody else thinks or says about you. You are not even what you think or say about yourself. You are who God says you are! The only one who is qualified to say who you are is the One who created you!

When an artist creates a masterpiece, it can be interpreted in many different ways by many different people. But the only one that knows the true significance and intended purpose of the piece is the artist. It is the artist that knows each and every building block used to create the piece.

God put you together cell by cell. He created your DNA, He knows the number of hairs on your head, He knows your heart and your mind. He knows the family that He chose for you to be born into. He planned the exact place and time that you would be born. And He put you on earth at that time and in that place for a specific purpose, which only He knows. You will only really know your value and your worth when you believe what God says about you.

> For you created my inmost being; you knit me together in my mother's womb. I praise you because I am fearfully and wonderfully made; your works are wonderful, I know that full well. My frame was not hidden from you when I was made in the secret place. When I was woven together in the depths of the earth, your eyes saw my unformed body. All the days ordained

for me were written in your book before one of them came to be. (Psalm 139:13–16)

What labels are being used to define you (i.e. parent, boss, student, athlete, smart, funny, your personality type—sanguine [orange], melancholy [green], etc.)?

Is there an area of your life (i.e. a person, a title, a position of authority, your ability to play a sport or music, what you look like, etc.) that would cause you to question who you are or your value if it was taken away?

Journal any additional messages, thoughts, or ideas that God has placed on your heart:

Prayer Circles

Use your prayer circles for the labels that you identified. Surrender them in prayer and ask God to help you replace these labels with truth. If you couldn't think of any labels or areas that you may be putting your identity in, instead of Christ, then ask Him to reveal any areas that may be hidden.

Details: Details:

Bible Verse: Bible Verse:

Identity—Day 2

The Bible tells us that we have been adopted into God's family through Jesus Christ: We are co-heirs with Christ!

> Because you are his sons, God sent the Spirit of his Son into our hearts, the Spirit who calls out, *"Abba,* Father." So you are no longer a slave, but God's child; and since you are his child, God has made you also an heir. (Galatians 4:6–7)

> Even before he made the world, God loved us and chose us in Christ to be holy and without fault in his eyes. God decided in advance to adopt us into his own family by bringing us to himself through Jesus Christ. This is what he wanted to do, and it gave him great pleasure. So we praise God for the glorious grace he has poured out on us who belong to his dear Son. (Ephesians 1:4–6 NLT)

To be adopted back in Roman times was very costly. When the Apostle Paul (who wrote Galatians, Ephesians and Romans as well as several other books of the New Testament) was speaking about being adopted and becoming an heir, he was speaking in a way that the Gentiles (non-Jewish people) could understand. Once adopted, everything in your past was cleared and could not be reversed. A natural born son could be killed but an adopted son could not. Once you became a part of the family you could not be separated. And you would receive the same inheritance as the natural born son.

Romans 8:14,17 tell us that those led by the Spirit of God are the children of God, and as His children, we are heirs of God and co-heirs with Christ. We become part of God's family and nothing can separate us from Him. Our past has been cleared and cannot be reversed. We receive the same glorious, eternal inheritance that Jesus has received! Let the enormity of this settle deep in your soul!

Regardless of your background or the circumstances of your natural born family, as a follower of Jesus Christ you are a child of God. You have a place where you belong completely and are loved unconditionally. You belong to the holy and righteous family of God—made holy and righteous through the only possible way, the blood of Jesus Christ!

> God made him who had no sin to be sin for us, so that in him we might become the righteousness of God. (2 Corinthians 5:21)

How does it make you feel to know you are adopted into God's family, a co-heir with Jesus Christ?

Do you have any struggles in accepting this reality? If so, what are they?

Journal any additional messages, thoughts, or ideas that God has placed on your heart:

Prayer Circles

Based on your revelations, reflections, thoughts, and ideas, what or whom can you circle in prayer?

Details: Details:

Bible Verse: Bible Verse:

Identity—Day 3

As a Christian, adopted into God's family, we take the name of Jesus. We become carriers of His identity.

In Steven Furtick's book, *(UN)QUALIFIED*, he explains that the commandment in Exodus 20:7 that states we should not take the Lord's name in vain is more than using His name disrespectfully in our vocabulary. It is about how we are carrying His name. When we are not believing and living in a way that reflects His identity—we are taking His name in vain. When we contradict what God says about us, we are taking His name in vain; treating His name as empty and hollow.[37]

We need to stop looking at who we are not and look at who Jesus is—we will not be able to reach our true potential otherwise.

Jesus was fearless, selfless, compassionate, and generous.

We need to remember that when Jesus came to earth He was born a man. When He walked the earth, He was not being fearless, selfless, compassionate, and generous as God. He did not resist temptation or perform miracles as God. When He resisted the temptations of Satan in the desert, when He healed the sick, fed thousands of people with a few small fish and seven loaves of bread, turned water into wine, walked on water, and raised the dead—He did all of this *as a man* with the power of the Holy Spirit within Him, just like you and I have within us. **He showed us what can be done when we are confident in our true identity**.

When you know *who* created you, *who* called you, *who* loves you completely and perfectly, and *whose* family you belong to then you can confidently carry His name as you step into the plan and purpose that God has for you.

Are you living in a way that reflects who Jesus is? If not, don't start chastising your actions and striving for behavior modification. This is about your identity, not your actions.

In the journal section, list one or two actions that you think do not reflect the identity of Jesus. Be vulnerable and meditate on the "why" behind the actions. Keep asking "why?" until you get down to the root cause. This may take some deep reflection; don't just skim the surface, allow yourself to dive deep.

Journal the results of your reflection and any additional messages, thoughts, or ideas that God has placed on your heart:

Prayer Circles

Based on any areas that were revealed in the exercise above, or any additional thoughts, what can you circle in prayer?

Details: Details:

Bible Verse: Bible Verse:

Identity—Day 4

One action that we often do, that doesn't reflect the fearlessness and selflessness of Jesus, is stop ourselves from dreaming or acting on our dreams because we think "Who am I to do that?"

When God first downloaded this book into my head and my heart, I was super excited. As time went on, I started to repeatedly have thoughts that questioned why I was doing this. *Why am I trying to write a book? Who am I to think that people will want to read what I have to say?* I would compare myself to great authors and Bible teachers and think: *Who do I think I am?*

Then, all the teachings that God has given me through His Word and numerous people would kick in (I can't emphasize enough how important it is to have God's Word hidden in your heart for these moments), and I would stop those thoughts and say: *Who am I? I am a daughter of the King! I am a child of God! I am created and chosen by God Himself! I am a vessel for Holy Spirit to guide and lead and use as He sees fit.*

So are you! You are chosen by God Himself—a son or daughter of the King!

Some better questions for us to ask when we are having doubts about what God has called us to do are: "Who am I to question what the Creator of the universe has created?"; "Who am I to question what God is asking me to do?"

God doesn't make mistakes—the way He made you is good!

We are insulting and dishonoring God when we say that we are not good enough for the tasks that He has assigned us to do or the dreams that He has planted in our hearts.

Not only that, we are saying that what Jesus did on the cross is not enough for us! Jesus died to take the penalty for our sins so that we could become the righteousness of God. Then He rose again and left us with the Holy Spirit who lives inside of us. Jesus said that we will do greater things than He did because He was going to the Father (John 14:12) so that we could have the power of the Holy Spirit in us (Acts 1:8). Always with us. Always ready to help us, guide us, teach us, strengthen us, comfort us.

He provides us the gift of *ultimate power* that equips us to do whatever He asks us to do—but we say we can't do it. We put limits on ourselves that do not exist. And when we put limits on our dreams, we will not fulfill the full purpose that God has for us. We are limiting the impact that we can have on eternity.

What dream has God put in your heart that you have not acted on because you don't think you are qualified, or ready, or because you feel it is too big (and maybe you are scared of what will happen if you succeed)?

Journal any dreams that God has placed on your heart:

Prayer Circles

Based on your dream(s), what or whom can you circle in prayer?

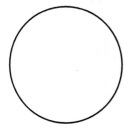

Details: Details:

Bible Verse: Bible Verse:

Identity—Day 5

Your life's work is to focus on knowing Jesus, to have a personal relationship with Him; to devote your own life to pleasing God; learning to see as He sees, think as He thinks, and love as He loves.

> [For my determined purpose is] that I may know Him [that I may progressively become more deeply and intimately acquainted with Him, perceiving and recognizing and understanding the wonders of His Person more strongly and more clearly], and that I may in that same way come to know the power outflowing from His resurrection [which it exerts over believers]. (Philippians 3:10 AMP)

To quote a couple of my favorite teachers: Steven Furtick said it this way, "When you discover who God is, you discover who you are.";[38] and Joyce Meyer says, "Righteousness is knowing who you are in Christ. You can't have peace without righteousness and you can't have joy without peace."[39]

Without a personal relationship with Jesus Christ, knowing Him deeply and intimately, and recognizing and understanding the wonders of His Person, you will limit your opportunity to experience and express love, joy, and peace.

When you have your identity in Christ, you will be confident because you put your confidence in Him; you won't care what other people think. You will understand that your weakness does not disqualify you; God does not call the qualified, He qualifies the called. You will dream big and live those dreams (Psalm 18:19)! You will stop trying to impress people, instead your desire will be to impress God. You will stop comparing, stop trying to do what somebody else is doing and do what God is asking you to do. You will trust God and have peace that surpasses understanding (Philippians 4:7). You will live a life worthy of your calling (Ephesians 4:1)—like what Jesus did on the cross was enough for you. You will confidently, boldly, and humbly accept the tasks that God assigns you; recognizing that you are God's masterpiece that He created in Christ Jesus to do the good works that God prepared in advance for you to do (Ephesians 2:10). You will live like you are completely and perfectly loved. You will realize that your significance, value, and worth come from God;

not from what you do, what you have, or what somebody else says or thinks about you. You will realize that God set you apart and created you specifically, intentionally, and uniquely for such a time as this.

Where are you at in your relationship with Jesus? Do you truly know Him? Do you know what God's Word says about Him and about you?

Do you have the joy and peace that come from having confidence in who you are in Christ?

Journal any additional messages, thoughts, or ideas that God has placed on your heart:

Prayer Circles

Based on your reflections, thoughts, or ideas, what or whom can you circle in prayer?

Details: Details:

Bible Verse: Bible Verse:

Identity—Day 6

What is keeping you from walking in the true identity that Christ died to give you?

My journey has led me to realize four key factors that keep us from stepping into our full identity in Christ. We have pondered these factors in more detail in the first four sections. Let's recap.

The first factor that will keep you from receiving your true identity in Christ is:

1. **Not accepting God's never-ending, never-changing, never-failing love for you.**

   In his devotional, *Devoted: Transform Your Life One Day at a Time*, Leon Fontaine said it so well, "You see, what matters most is not how much you love God. It's finding out how much He loves you. Focus on your love for Him and you're always trying. **Focus on His love for you and your life will change!**"[40] When you start to see yourself the way Jesus sees you, through eyes of unfailing love, your perspective on everything will change and you will live your life differently. And God doesn't just love you as part of a large group of people that He loves, He loves you uniquely! Not long ago I realized that I always thought of God's love as a corporate love; I thought that He loves me the same as everybody else. But He made each of us uniquely and He loves each of us uniquely, not more or less, but differently.

Ask God what He loves about you. Ask Him to be specific. Be alert and ready to receive His response. It may not come immediately and it may come in a variety of ways. Be sure to write it down when He responds— use the journal section to capture any immediate responses.

In *Love—Day 1*, we used 1 Corinthians 13:4–8 as our foundational definition of love and you reflected on how your feelings about His love for you align with this definition. Re-read these verses and capture how your feelings about His love for you align with this definition now. Has it changed?

> Love is patient, love is kind. It does not envy, it does not boast, it is not proud. It does not dishonor others, it is not self-seeking, it is not easily angered, it keeps no record of wrongs. Love does not delight in evil but rejoices with the truth. It always protects, always trusts, always hopes, always perseveres. Love never fails. (1 Corinthians 13:4–8)

Journal any responses, thoughts, or ideas that God has placed on your heart:

Prayer Circles

Based on your reflections, thoughts, or ideas, what or whom can you circle in prayer?

Details: Details:

Bible Verse: Bible Verse:

Identity—Day 7

The second factor that will keep you from living in your true identity in Christ is:

2. **Not trusting God with 100% of your life**.

    Our trust will continue to grow as we experience new opportunities to trust God, but we need to have hearts that are willing to surrender in every aspect of our life (our children, our relationships, our finances, our decisions, etc.); we can't pick and choose which areas we will trust Him with. We need to decide that we are going to believe God for who He is, not just for what He does or does not do. God loves you, He wants nothing but the best for you, and He sees from the beginning to the end: He has <u>all</u> the information required to make the best decisions. You can confidently surrender every facet of your life to God without the fear of being let down. God is faithful and He will never betray your trust. He is the only one who is able to do exceedingly abundantly, immeasurably, infinitely more than all you ask or imagine (Ephesians 3:20)!

Trust in the LORD with all your heart and lean not on your own understanding; in all your ways submit to him, and he will make your paths straight. (Proverbs 3:5–6)

Choose one area of your life that you have not yet completely trusted to God and surrender it to Him right now; release control into His hands. Let Him guide you to do your part and then leave His part to Him. Write a prayer of surrender and use this prayer as one of your prayer circles.

Journal any additional messages, thoughts, or ideas that God has placed on your heart:

Prayer Circles

Based on your reflections, thoughts, or ideas, what areas of surrender can you circle in prayer?

Details: Details:

Bible Verse: Bible Verse:

Identity—Day 8

The third obstacle that will keep you from embracing your true identity in Christ is:

3. **Pride**

   The struggle to relinquish control, not wanting to look bad, and caring about what other people think, are just a few of the seeds of pride that will keep you distant from God. This obstacle is huge because it is so prevalent. Pride can masquerade as so many different things. Some things that God needs to root out of your heart will be more difficult than others. Some might need a delicate touch with tweezers to remove, while others may require a jackhammer! Let Him do the work in you—open your heart and mind to receive what He is showing you. Keep your heart pliable and your spirit teachable. Ask Him to show you the areas where you are being prideful and then listen to what He has to say. God cannot transform who you pretend to be. Let Him strip away the masks so that He can deal directly with the real you.

God wants you to know Him. Pride is a barrier that will keep you from developing a close personal relationship with Jesus.

Remember, a truly humble heart comes from the transformation that occurs as you find your identity in Christ. We are simply developing our awareness of the pride barriers that exist so we can look to Jesus to help us break them down; He knows we can't do it on our own. That is why He tells us to let Him help us.

"Take my yoke upon you and learn from me, for I am gentle and humble in heart, and you will find rest for your souls." (Matthew 11:29)

Write a prayer to God that confesses any areas of pride that you may have been hanging on to (or may have just realized). Ask Him to help you with these areas. Express your longing to know Him more and your desire for all barriers that are keeping you from knowing Him to be gone.

Journal any additional messages, thoughts, or ideas that God has placed on your heart:

Prayer Circles

Based on your reflections, thoughts, or ideas, what or whom can you circle in prayer?

Details: Details:

Bible Verse: Bible Verse:

Identity—Day 9

The fourth factor that will keep you from receiving your true identity in Christ is:

4. **Not planting yourself in the House of God**.

> We get to know Jesus better personally through a strong community of believers that are all learning together. Each person's relationship with Jesus is unique and the accumulation of these unique relationships provides all of us with a more in-depth and well-rounded understanding of who Jesus is. It deepens our corporate relationship with Jesus as well as each individual relationship. Church allows us to know the fullness of Jesus that we can't know on our own—giving us the power, together with all the Lord's holy people, to grasp His love for us (Ephesians 3:18) and, as a result, to put our trust completely in Him.

Church will help you find your identity in Christ, and in turn, knowing who you are in Christ will impact how you see church and your role within it. This is one of the beautiful mysteries of God—He opens our eyes to things that we don't even realize we are blind to!

If you are not planted (meaning you are attending but not contributing) in a good, Jesus-centered, Bible-based church, make that your first fearless step towards receiving your true identity in Christ (or if you do not currently have a church to call home, then make finding one your first fearless step). Join a team to serve on or sign up to be part of a connect group. Don't wait until you accept God's love for you, trust Him completely and have cleaned up your prideful ways! **Do this first!** If you wait until the other factors are all dealt with, then it will never happen. Remember, our sanctification is a life-long process. Being planted in church will provide a support system for you and is vital to that process. Together we become what we cannot be alone.

Use your prayer circles today to help you take this next step. Pray for God to lead you to the right people in church (and the right church if necessary). Pray that He will bring new friendships and give you the strength and courage to reach out and get involved in your church.

The righteous will flourish like a palm tree, they will grow like a cedar of Lebanon; planted in the house of the LORD, they will flourish in the courts of our God. (Psalm 92:12–13)

"How awesome is this place! This is none other than the house of God; this is the gate of heaven." (Genesis 28:17)

Journal any additional messages, thoughts, or ideas that God has placed on your heart:

Prayer Circles

Based on your reflections, thoughts, or ideas, what or whom can you circle in prayer?

Details: Details:

Bible Verse: Bible Verse:

Identity—Day 10 (Conclusion)

When overcoming any of the obstacles that are keeping you from confidently walking in your Christ-like identity, you don't need to—and in fact you can't—do it on your own. You need God's grace (His unmerited favor) to sustain you and help you. God's grace frees you to receive your true identity. Let His grace wash over you, saturate you, cleanse you, and transform you.

God will reveal what He needs to reveal at the right time; it will be a progressive revelation. God will dig deeper when you are ready. Following Jesus and being transformed into His image is a life-long process, not a one-time event. But God will use you while you are still a work in progress, every step along the way.

Our job is to be obedient to what He asks us to do and let Him deal with the outcome. This is part of the journey of getting to know Him better. With each step of obedience, He reveals Himself to us more and more! Trust in His promises and don't worry about the outcome. Even if the outcome is not what you expect, the results within you that come from the process of your obedience will be more than you could possibly imagine. You will be transformed into the image of Christ—gradually becoming more like Him!

> Nothing between us and God, our faces shining with the brightness of his face. And so we are transfigured much like the Messiah, our lives gradually becoming brighter and more beautiful as God enters our lives and we become like him. (2 Corinthians 3:18 MSG)

Being confident in Christ does not equate to being arrogant. It doesn't mean you think you are better than other people or that what you are called to do is more important than what others are called to do. When you realize your own value and worth, you will also see the value and worth of others. We have each been created and put on this planet at this particular time with unique gifts, personalities, talents, and abilities to do our part to build eternity. We must press on courageously and persistently to reach the goal for which God has called us heavenward in Christ Jesus.

Not that I have already obtained all this, or have already arrived at my goal, but I press on to take hold of that for which Christ Jesus took hold of me. Brothers and sisters, I do not consider myself yet to have taken hold of it. But one thing I do: Forgetting what is behind and straining toward what is ahead, I press on toward the goal to win the prize for which God has called me heavenward in Christ Jesus. (Philippians 3:12–14)

Just before Jesus ascended into heaven He left us with the Great Commission. He very simply told us what our purpose is—to make disciples of all nations (Matthew 28:19–20). We all have the same purpose—to help people become disciples of Jesus. How you are called to fulfill this purpose is your own unique journey.

The Bible tells us in Ephesians 6:17, that part of the armor of God is the sword of the Spirit, which is the Word of God. It also tells us that Jesus is the Word (John 1:1,14). As you dive deeper into the Word of God and pursue a relationship with Jesus, you will claim your new creation nature and walk confidently as a child of God and co-heir with Jesus. With your identity in Christ, the love of Jesus will flow through you as a polished arrow that penetrates even the hardened hearts of those around you. And your mouth will be a sharpened sword that proclaims the Word of God and displays His splendor through the word of your testimony.

YOU CAN DO IT! As a Christian that carries the name of Christ, step boldly and confidently into the identity that Jesus died for you to have. Pursue the dreams God has placed in your heart! Say YES to everything God asks you to do, knowing that you can trust Him completely because He loves you so very much!

God called you and chose you to display His splendor! He has equipped you as a warrior for His Kingdom. You are ready for battle; prepared to demolish any strongholds that are keeping you from the spacious life that God has called you to! As you walk confidently in the victory that Jesus Christ has given you, the way you live your life and the words you speak will be weapons to display God's glory and majesty, the magnificence and wonder of our Lord Jesus Christ!

Will you do the part that God has asked you to do?

Will you rise up and do battle?

Will you step into all that God has planned for you?

> Listen to me, you islands;
>   hear this, you distant nations:
> Before I was born the LORD called me;
>   from my mother's womb he has spoken my name.
> He made my mouth like a sharpened sword,
>   in the shadow of his hand he hid me;
> he made me into a polished arrow
>   and concealed me in his quiver.
> He said to me, "You are my servant,
>   Israel, in whom I will display my splendor." (Isaiah 49: 1–3)

Journal any final thoughts that God has placed on your heart about your identity in Christ:

Prayer Circles

Based on your reflections, thoughts, or ideas, what or who can you circle in prayer?

Details: Details:

Bible Verse: Bible Verse:

Notes

1   Mark Batterson, *The Circle Maker: Praying Circles Around Your Biggest Dreams And Greatest Fears* (Grand Rapids, Michigan: Zondervan, 2011), 9–11.

2   Melanie Mitchell, *I Don't Think So: Leaving Behind The Why Me Mentality And Taking Control Of Your Life* (Italy: Evangelista Media, 2013), 55.

3   Mitchell, *I Don't Think So*, 97.

4   The Blue Letter Bible, s.v. "peripoieō," accessed February 9, 2017, https://www.blueletterbible.org/lang/lexicon/lexicon.cfm?strongs=G4046&t=NIV.

5   study. Dictionary.com. *Dictionary.com Unabridged.* Random House, Inc. http://www.dictionary.com/browse/study (accessed: February 16, 2017).

6   The Blue Letter Bible, s.v. "tērēo," accessed February 9, 2017, https://www.blueletterbible.org/lang/lexicon/lexicon.cfm?Strongs=G5083&t=NIV.

7   The Blue Letter Bible, s.v. "theōreō," accessed February 9, 2017, https://www.blueletterbible.org/lang/lexicon/lexicon.cfm?strongs=G2334&t=NIV.

8   Joyce Meyer, *Knowing Who You Are in Christ: See Yourself as God Sees You* (Joyce Meyer Ministries), CD.

9   The Blue Letter Bible, s.v. "ginōskō," accessed February 9, 2017, https://www.blueletterbible.org/lang/lexicon/lexicon.cfm?t=kjv&strongs=g1097.

10   Jewish Virtual Library: A Project of AICE, "Hallel", http://www.jewishvirtuallibrary.org/hallel (accessed: February 17, 2017).; Benedict XVI, General Audience (Libreria Editrice Vaticana, 2011), https://w2.vatican.va/content/benedict-xvi/en/audiences/2011/documents/hf ben-xvi aud 20111019.html (accessed: February 17, 2017).

11   The Blue Letter Bible, s.v. "batach," accessed February 9, 2017, https://www.blueletterbible.org/lang/lexicon/lexicon.cfm?Strongs=H982&t=NIV.

12   trust. Dictionary.com. *Dictionary.com Unabridged.* Random House, Inc. http://www.dictionary.com/browse/trust (accessed: February 16, 2017).; American Dictionary of the English Language, "Webster's Dictionary 1828," accessed February 9, 2017, http://webstersdictionary1828.com/Dictionary/trust.

13   The Blue Letter Bible, s.v. "kol," accessed February 9, 2017, https://www.blueletterbible.org/lang/lexicon/lexicon.cfm?Strongs=H3605&t=NIV.

14   John Bevere, *Good or God: Why Good Without God Isn't Enough* (Palmer Lake, CO: Messenger International, Inc., 2015), 59–61.

15 C.S. Lewis, *Mere Christianity: The Complete C.S. Lewis Signature Classics* (New York: HarperCollins Publishers, 2002), 103.

16 humility. Dictionary.com. *Dictionary.com Unabridged*. Random House, Inc. http://www.dictionary.com/browse/humility (accessed: February 16, 2017).

17 humble. Dictionary.com. *Collins English Dictionary - Complete & Unabridged 10th Edition*. HarperCollins Publishers. http://www.dictionary.com/browse/humble (accessed: February 16, 2017).

18 The Blue Letter Bible, s.v. "praotēs," accessed February 9, 2017, https://www.blueletterbible.org/lang/lexicon/lexicon.cfm?Strongs=G4236&t=NKJV.

19 W.E. Vine, Merrill F. Unger, William White, Jr., *Vine's Complete Expository Dictionary of Old and New Testament Words* (Nashville, Tennessee: Thomas Nelson, Inc., 1996), 401.

20 Lewis, *Mere Christianity*, 108.

21 Rick Warren, *The Purpose Driven Life: What on Earth Am I Here For?* (Grand Rapids, Michigan: Zondervan, 2002), 148.

22 Steven Furtick, *(UN)QUALIFIED: How God Uses Broken People To Do Big Things* (Colorado Springs, Colorado: Multnomah Books, 2016), 14.

23 Lewis, *Mere Christianity*, 107.

24 Lewis, *Mere Christianity*, 176.

25 Chad Brand, Charles Draper, Archie England, Steve Bond, E. Ray Clendenen, Trent C. Butler, eds., *Holman Illustrated Bible Dictionary* (Nashville, Tennessee: Holman Bible Publishers, 2003), 793.

26 Audrey Meisner, *Like Yourself, Love Your Life: Overcome Big Mistakes & Celebrate Your True Beauty* (Newburg, PA: Milestones International Publishers, 2011), 87–88.

27 Hear it First, LLC, "10 Powerful Quotes from the Movie Facing the Giants," last modified September 24, 2014, http://www.hearitfirst.com/news/10-powerful-quotes-from-the-movie-facing-the-giants.

28 Henry K. Ripplinger, *The Angelic Occurrence* (Canada: Pio-Seelos Books, 2013), 486.

29 Lewis, *Mere Christianity*, 105.

30 Lewis, *Mere Christianity*, 164.

31   The Blue Letter Bible, s.v. "ekklēsia," accessed February 9, 2017, https://www.
     blueletterbible.org/lang/lexicon/lexicon.cfm?Strongs=G1577&t=NIV.

32   Chad Brand, Charles Draper, Archie England, Steve Bond, E. Ray Clendenen,
     Trent C. Butler, *eds.*, *Holman Illustrated Bible Dictionary* (Nashville, Tennessee:
     Holman Bible Publishers, 2003), 295.

33   Brand, Draper, England, Bond, Clendenen, Butler, *eds.*, *Holman Illustrated Bible
     Dictionary*, 296.

34   *Life Application Study Bible, New International Version* (Grand Rapids, Michigan:
     Tyndale House Publishers, Inc. and Zondervan, 2005), 1986.

35   F.F. Bruce, *ed.*, *One-Volume Illustrated Edition Zondervan Bible Commentary* (Grand
     Rapids, Michigan: Zondervan, 2008), 1248.

36   Ecclesia Bible Society, *The Voice Bible: Step into the Story of Scripture* (Nashville,
     Tennessee: Thomas Nelson, Inc., 2012), 1445.

37   Furtick, *(UN)QUALIFIED*, 63–64.

38   Furtick, *(UN)QUALIFIED*, 67.

39   Joyce Meyer, *Confidence to be an Individual: Confidence: Freedom to be Yourself*
     (Joyce Meyer Ministries, 2002), audio.

40   Leon Fontaine, *Devoted: Transform Your Life One Day at a Time: October–December
     2014* (Lethbridge, Alberta: Miracle Channel, 2014), Monday, November 10.